December 4, 2010

Dearest Kyle,
I hope you enjoy this little
story. I also hope it will
encourage you to set your sights
on adventures – big adventures.
you will always be among
those I love.

much love +
Light,

Janet

IN SECRET AND SHADOWS

IN SECRET AND SHADOWS

DISCOVERING LIGHT *in the* SOUTH *of* FRANCE

JANET RENU PULLEN

BALBOA.
PRESS

A DIVISION OF HAY HOUSE

Balboa Press books may be ordered through booksellers or by contacting:

Balboa Press
A Division of Hay House
1663 Liberty Drive
Bloomington, IN 47403
www.balboapress.com
1-(877) 407–4847

ISBN: 978-1-4525-0018-8 (sc)
ISBN: 978-1-4525-0019-5 (e)

Printed in the United States of America

Balboa Press rev. date: 9/29/2010

To Didier, of course.

NOTE *to the* READER

In Secret and Shadows was inspired by a true story. The names of some characters have been changed and time sequences altered for literary purposes. The story is not intended to be a history lesson. It is rather an account of my own mystical journey, my own individual search for truth. My greatest hope is that *In Secret and Shadows* will encourage readers to courageously set out on their own Grail Quest, putting aside all maps of the known world and trusting instead their own inner navigation system to illuminate the path.

Janet Renu Pullen
San Jose, California
May 17, 2010

ACKNOWLEDGEMENTS

For their love, support, inspiration and guidance in the development of this book I want to sincerely thank the following; my sweet friend and collaborator Chris Plant, who stayed with me every step of the way, Julia Struyck who was there in the beginning and continued to be lovingly present as Alicia even in Santiago, Anne Hill who provided her cozy upstairs room for our late night discussions at 8 *rue Louis Bleriot*, Tana Burden who often came along, my sister Julie Newcomb who put down what she was doing and came to France to see what I was talking about, Carol Smith who encouraged me to write the story and helped me to understand, Bill and Michael who listened to me read the first chapter of the manuscript while sipping *Banyuls* in the sun-splashed bar of *Les Templiers* in the joyous seaside town of Collioure, dearest Deetsie Herbine who reminded me that chickens lay eggs not people, Jon Graham who introduced me to the Templar, Lyall Watson and Marcel Proust, then later convinced me that my own story had merit, Claire Gerus who tenderly took the manuscript apart, polished it up and put it back together, the book's designer Beta Vitale with her exceptional eye for detail, beauty and mystery, my California Soul Group; Ruth Litwin, Barrie Cress, Diane Portnoy and Martha Weiner, who always see the best in me, encouraging early readers; Elizabeth Pomada, Margaret Starbird, Douglas Preston, Paula Sneddon, Stan Litwin, Jon Cress, Wayne Levenfeld, Prem Sobel, Karen Aiken, Christine Warren, and Kate Feldman, the late night midwives; Dee Kennedy, John Wiggin, Sumaiya Malik and Cheryl Richardson whose timely siren song brought me to Balboa Press.

Finally I offer my deepest gratitude to my darling Rachel and Nicholas who thrived despite their mother having been lost in the foothills of the Pyrénées for the better part of five years.

IN SECRET *and* SHADOWS

Secrets in Shadow,
oasis of Light.
sparks off its water,
see into the night.
Tearing from darkness all of its covers.
Finding the lost and forgotten lovers.

John Wiggin

TABLE *of* CONTENTS

INTRODUCTION

In the early summer of 325 AD, nearly 300 men convened in a large, marble-columned hall at the edge of a lake in the small Byzantine town of Nicea. The specific mission of the attendees of this council was to define a religion that would unite the sprawling Roman Empire under one supreme god.

By Imperial order, messengers had carried more than 1,800 invitations across the vast Empire. Those invited, while professing widely differing beliefs, all shared in common the Christian title of "bishop". Fewer than 400 of the invitees actually answered the Imperial summons. Those who did attend came mostly from the east: Alexandria, Cyprus, Egypt, Persia, Libya, and Palestine. Many in attendance were learned, finely dressed intellectuals; others had spent their lives in desert caves subsisting on roots and locusts.

Presiding over the council was the Roman Emperor, Constantine, a ruthless, superstitious megalomaniac with a violent temper—a man who had executed his own son on dubious charges and had his wife boiled in oil. He arrived at the council in a purple silk robe ablaze with jewels and gold embroidery, a tiara on his head and the unshakable conviction that the source of his imperial authority came from Above.

At the commencement of the council the determined Constantine stood to address the bishops. A hush fell on the hall and all eyes were riveted on the Roman Emperor. Speaking in Latin, the language of the court, and without attempting to disguise the threat beneath his words, Constantine began, "I entreat you beloved ministers of God to remove the causes of dissension among you and to establish unity and peace."

In a dramatic gesture, he then took a stack of parchment and letters previously sent to him from bishops across the empire detailing their disputes and threw them onto a fire built in the center of the hall for this specific purpose.

Seven weeks later, on July 25, a solemn banquet ended the Council. With all bitter quarrels about doctrine resolved, all vicious arguments decided, all dissent at last silenced, the Council of Bishops returned to Constantine what he had intended—an official state church. It consisted of both an ideology and a hierarchal structure of clergy and civil servants that would ensure the security and stability of the Roman Empire.

The council of Nicea concluded that henceforth there would be one Church, one single path to salvation, one creed and one authoritarian god who required absolute obedience. No further debate on any of these issues would be tolerated.

The orthodox Christian doctrine of the new Church had been arduously arrived at and was precisely defined. It eliminated completely the symbol of the Divine Feminine, central to every spiritual tradition of the ancient world. It melded instead all forms and images of the male gods into one singular Supreme "God." This new supreme-being consisted of three aspects: God the Father, God the Son and the amorphous God the Holy Ghost. The historical Jesus was collapsed into the Divine Son. He was now determined to have been born of a virgin mother, crucified under Pontius Pilate and resurrected bodily from his tomb after three days' interment.

Four canonical gospels, edited to support the new orthodox ideology, were selected to represent the state religion from among the hundreds of early Christian writings in circulation at the time. By Imperial order, all books challenging these would be banned and thrown into the flames.

All Pagan temples were ordered closed and their treasures re-dedicated. The official Orthodox Church would henceforth control all spirituality. One could no longer aspire to an independent pursuit of truth and knowledge, individually seek enlightenment, or pursue a personal relationship with God. Any such efforts would now be termed "heresy," considered criminal activity and punishable by death. (The word "heresy" is from a Greek word meaning "choice.")

In all, the Council debated and resolved 84 subjects, including the establishment of the date Easter would be celebrated and the outlawing of reincarnation. The latter was thought to minimize the role of Jesus and diminish the unique nature of his Resurrection. The Emperor Constantine had recognized Christianity as a powerful means of unifying and conquering dissension within the faltering Roman Empire. Yet he himself was not baptized until he was on his deathbed a full twelve years later!

CHAPTER ONE

A Step Out of Time

To be initiated is to have the veils of ignorance torn away.

Lynn V. Andrews, *Star Woman*

IN THE LATE SUMMER of 1995, my husband, Bill, and I, with our two children, Rachel and Nicholas, moved to a small village outside the city of Toulouse, France. Each of us arrived with different objectives: Bill had come to France to work, my children had come to learn the language and expand their worldview beyond rural Pennsylvania, and I had come because, for as long as I could remember, it had been the only place I'd ever wanted to live.

The daydreams of my childhood were, for reasons I could not explain, colored in pastel images of France. As a child, while my girlfriends fantasized about grown-up lives in Barbie kitchens, I imagined myself moving through charming French landscapes, parasol in hand. In my mind, I wandered the early morning markets on the medieval boulevards of the Left Bank and boated on the river Seine. Long before I had ever crossed the Atlantic, I had strolled along the Champs-Elysées and basked in the perfumed afternoon sunshine of the Luxembourg and Tuileries Gardens.

When I entered my teens, my dreams became more sophisticated. I imagined visiting the Louvre, the Musée D'Orsay, the Eiffel Tower and the Cathedral of Notre-Dame. I pictured myself drinking sweet, thick coffee from tiny cups in the cafes of Montmartre and tanning beneath the summer's sun on the beaches of St. Tropez.

While apparently enjoying burgers and shakes with my high school girlfriends, I was secretly oceans away in a land of freshly baked *baguettes*, exotic cheeses, rich red wines, cognac and champagne. When I should have been paying attention in math class, I was staring out the window dreaming of Joan of Arc, Renoir, Monet, Hemingway, and Gertrude Stein. To me, France held charms both ancient and modern, and within its borders lay everything I longed to experience one day.

Perhaps because of my lifelong romance with France, I naively expected my transition to its shores to be smooth as silk. I had never even considered that I could become a victim of culture shock. As a result, I was completely unprepared for what transpired once I arrived, at age 42, with my family in tow.

It wasn't just that everyone in France spoke a language different from ours. It was that everything—absolutely everything—was unlike what we were used to: the texture of the air, the taste of the water, the color of the nighttime sky, the mistletoe in the trees, and the milk that needed no refrigeration. People spread chocolate on their bread instead of peanut butter. Stores were called *magasins*, sheets were *drapeaux*, and a dollar was a *franc* whose exchange rate fluctuated almost daily.

When I spoke on the phone to my friends and family in the States, I struggled to find the words to explain how odd I felt. "I feel like I'm stuck between radio band frequencies," I told my sister. "It's as if I'm no longer myself."

It was hard to believe that an eight-hour plane ride could have taken us into a world so different. In less than a day, none of us knew where we were or how to ask directions. The simplest things became difficult. Tasks that I had previously handled on autopilot now made me stop and think. Shopping for groceries, doing the laundry, and driving a car seemed to pose new challenges and require new skills.

One afternoon, while walking through the village market, I realized that I was hearing the voices of those around me as if I were underwater. I knew people were speaking—a mother to her child, the grocery clerk to a customer—but what they were saying was completely incomprehensible. It was an odd sensation and made me realize how much I had previously relied on my communication skills. In the States, I had spoken to everyone—neighbors I passed on the street, the postman, and the clerk at the dry cleaner's. In fact, I knew them all by name.

Now, unable to speak to others or understand what people were saying, I began to feel unsafe, handicapped. It was as if I had lost an important part of my personality, and now I wasn't sure what remained. Some days I felt I was alone with a stranger—me.

Time itself had dramatically altered. Not only had the hours I'd once slept now become the hours I was awake, but the very rhythms, the natural cycles, and the pace of my life became jumbled and disordered.

Perhaps most surprising, while the day and month on the calendar remained the same, I began to feel as if our move across the Atlantic Ocean had initiated a slide backward through time. It seemed to me that, while America had been rushing forward, France had been standing still.

This "standing still" both frustrated and intrigued me. The dreadfully slow line at the post office was a constant source of irritation. But at the end of our street, the remains of an ancient wall was converted into a flower box in which pastel-colored geraniums had been planted. I found this tableau totally charming, beautiful, and mysterious. I couldn't help but imagine what the wall had once been part of. Perhaps it was the château of a local nobleman arrested during the Revolution, or it may have been an ancient church, or a local inn where villagers had once gathered to share a glass of *vin de pays* on cold winter nights.

I suspected that in America the old wall would have been demolished, the worn stone thrown away, the space given over to some newer form of commerce. While progress, no doubt, was important, it seemed America had lost something of true value in its rush to modernity.

Our leased house just outside the city of Toulouse in the small village of Cugnaux was lovely, surrounded by gardens and sitting on the edge of a sixteenth-century château property. The enormous neighboring château, with its great shuttered windows and its towers looking down on our garden, was a constant reminder of how very much our lives had changed. Protected by a grove of ancient oak trees, the elegant neighboring structure stood as if completely unaware—or maybe just totally unconcerned—that a twentieth century was taking place around it.

As I pursued my new life in the shadow of the château, my daily responsibilities included getting my children off to school, seeing my husband off to work, and preparing meals for everyone when they returned home. With every day focused on such menial tasks, my new life left me with far more time on my hands than I had anticipated. After many years of participating in the "hurry up, get more" lifestyle of America, I could, for the first time in years, relish hours of free time.

For several months after our arrival, I was able by mid-afternoon to curl up in a comfortable chair in our garden and lose myself in a book I hadn't previously had time to pick up, much less read. After making my way through the Brontë sisters, Jane Austen, Charles Dickens, Thomas Hardy and Tolstoy, I decided to read English translations of French literature. I read Marcel Proust, Simone de Beauvoir, Victor Hugo, Alexander Dumas, John Paul Sartre and Voltaire.

Along with my survey of French literature, I also began to read my collection of French guidebooks and began making a list of the places I wanted to visit, a list that lengthened as the days went by.

As we started to settle in, my family and I began taking long drives every Sunday afternoon, and it was on these early adventures that we came to fully recognize the powerful contrast between past and present in our new surroundings. While today Toulouse is recognized worldwide as one of the European Union's leading centers of aerospace and electronic technologies, on its perimeter thrived a rich, ancient culture that had endured, despite time's ruthless battle for supremacy.

Away from the city, nothing appeared to have changed during the past several hundred years. Regardless of which direction we drove from Toulouse, we always wound up on tiny roads bordered by neat rows of poplar trees, where ancient villages of stone houses with warm red tile roofs sat shuttered against the hot afternoon sun. These charming, if rough-hewn, homes eventually gave way to endless fields of golden sunflowers and age-old vineyards of gnarled and tangled grapevines.

Often during our Sunday drives, we would stop at a cafe in one of the quaint little villages to taste the *vin de pays*. Sitting in the sunshine as we sipped the local vintage, we began to appreciate that the French do not ascribe to the theory that "new" means "better." We came to understand that the French way of life, which had at first seemed antiquated, was not the result of their culture having been left behind. It was actually the intended outcome of a carefully designed plan to preserve the past.

As each day passed, while I should have been feeling increasingly confident in my new life, I instead felt as if I were losing more and more of my familiar moorings. Perhaps it was the effect of my general disorientation and culture shock. Perhaps it was the consequence of my dawning recognition that France proudly embraced both past and present. Maybe it was due to our Sunday afternoon wine-tasting trips, or the continuing influence of the neighboring château.

Whatever the reason, I seemed to be steadily sliding farther and farther away from the boundaries of a recognizable and secure world, and found myself becoming increasingly anxious about it. Too much had changed, too quickly. I felt compelled to hold onto something familiar, but there didn't seem to be anything to hold onto.

It wasn't the same for Bill and the kids. Though they were also struggling to understand the language and the culture; Bill was engaged in an exciting new business venture and could communicate with his associates in both English and French. Rachel and Nicholas were at a French school making new friends every day, and learning the language from them.

One Sunday afternoon, while driving on the auto route heading toward the sea, Bill and I encountered a curious road sign that read, *Vous êtes en pays Cathare.* The translation was: "You are in the country of the Cathar." *What's a Cathar?* we wondered.

CHAPTER TWO

The Haunted Cathar Château of Montségur

To walk this road means to go contrary to the world
and to the notions of the reasonable and the probable.

Stephan Hoeller, *The Gnostic Jung*

A FEW DAYS LATER, Bill and I were having an aperitif with an
American couple who were packing up to return to the States. Ray and his
wife, Joan, had spent the past three years living in France but Ray's work
assignment had recently been completed and they were now reluctantly
heading home. Remembering the enigmatic road sign, we asked them if
they knew the meaning of the word, "Cathar."

"The Cathar were religious dissidents that lived around Toulouse in the
Middle Ages," replied Ray.

"You absolutely must visit the Cathar châteaux," Joan interrupted, clearly
eager to join the conversation. "They're extraordinary medieval buildings,
and all that remain of a fascinating period of French history."

As Joan refilled our glasses, Ray reached beneath their coffee table,
pulled out a *Michelin* map book, and began thumbing through its pages.

"Here they are," he announced, pointing to the tiny crosses dotted
throughout the Pyrénées Mountains. "These crosses mark the châteaux

where the medieval heretics, called the Cathar, lived. Do be sure to see them," Ray urged. "They're a must-see while you're here."

"And when you go," laughed Joan, "be sure to wear a good pair of hiking shoes. It's a long way to the top, but well worth the climb."

I was intrigued by what Ray and Joan had told us about the Cathar châteaux. And for some reason, the very idea of medieval French heretics fascinated me. Bill's workload, however, suddenly increased and we found it difficult to arrange a time to go. After waiting several frustrating weeks for his schedule to change, I decided that if I were to visit a Cathar château any time soon, I'd have to go on my own.

Despite my fear that I would get hopelessly lost, my curiosity eventually got the best of me, and one beautiful morning I asked Bill to map out the route to a Cathar château called Montségur.

"Are you sure you want to make this trip on your own?" Bill asked, trying unsuccessfully to mask his concern.

"I'd really rather be going with you," I confessed as I pulled some snacks out of the refrigerator and packed them into a bag. "But I don't want to wait any longer. I'll be fine and I promise to tell you everything over dinner."

Then, after dropping Bill off at work and the kids at school, I headed south. Although I had tried to convince Bill otherwise, I really wasn't very confident about taking this trip on my own.

But to my surprise, I had no trouble finding my way to the medieval Cathar château. The roads were well marked and Bill's directions were clear.

It wasn't until I'd pulled up next to the towering pinnacle of rock, however, that I remembered Joan's warning about the steep climb. The drive to Montségur had been easy, but I could see clearly from the base of the mountain that the hike up to the château's ruin at the top would not be.

There were no other cars in the parking lot and no one else on the path as I began my climb. Why? I asked myself as I struggled up the cliff, would anyone ever want to live in a place that was this hard to get to?

While it had been months since I'd first heard the word, "Cathar," I had learned little about them, other than that some of them had lived in the château at the top of this impossible mountain. Now, as I climbed up the rugged, and at times demanding, path that wound around strewn rocks and through a tangle of pungent boxwood, I wondered whether what awaited me at the top could possibly be worth my extreme efforts to get there.

After climbing for almost an hour, I arrived, breathless but exultant, at the summit of the mountain. Looking at the soaring walls of the awesome château of Montségur looming before me, I stopped to catch my breath, spellbound.

I was at least a thousand feet high, above the clouds and able to see for miles in every direction. The extensive vista was spectacular. The undulating foothills of the surrounding Pyrénées were abloom, boasting a lustrous array of colorful wildflowers. Beneath me green velvet valleys and rocky limestone hills, all rounded and crumbling at their peaks, stretched out for as far as I could see.

The vivid beauty of the view was strangely moving and somehow suggestive of an unknown place I'd previously been but long ago forgotten. I could hear the copper bells of nearby grazing dairy cows ringing softly. Otherwise, there was a profound silence.

OK, I conceded, struck by the incredible vista. Maybe I can see why someone would want to live up here, after all.

As I walked through the entrance of the château and into its huge, roofless skeleton, without warning, my calf muscles cramped and then melted beneath me. Unable to resist, I let myself sink down onto the moist earth, instinctively closing my eyes against the brilliant sunlight.

And then something unimaginable happened. I intended to rest for only just a moment. Instead, I drifted off into a strange, dreamlike state.

As I lay with my eyes closed on the sun-warmed ground, Montségur suddenly came alive. Voices, laughter and the sounds of playful dogs filled the previously silent air. Where moments before there had been no one, there were now dozens of curious people moving about, seemingly engaged in routine, everyday activities.

A small group of women sat together spinning dark-colored wool. Another group, singing softly as they worked, labored beside a huge, simmering pot. A plume of sweet, earthy-smelling smoke rose from the pot and mingled with the wind. Beyond the enormous gate, a third group of both men and women gathered around a man playing an unfamiliar stringed instrument.

If it weren't for the unworldly light illuminating the entire scene, it would have seemed as if I were witnessing a historical reenactment created for school children on a field trip. "I must be dreaming," I assured myself. "I've simply fallen asleep and I'm dreaming. I am dreaming, aren't I? But then why do I feel so completely awake?"

Walking beneath the far side of the château wall was a young girl wearing a blue cloak. She was accompanied by a man, who unlike all the others, was dressed in what appeared to be a soldier's uniform.

In contrast with those around him, the man appeared exhausted, his face dirty and unshaven, his clothing disheveled, his gait labored and slow. His eyes, however, were remarkably alert and his attentive gaze focused sharply on the young girl as if he expected something from her.

The girl herself was very beautiful, and seemed to radiate an unworldly vitality. She also exuded a strange sweetness that flooded my heart so intensely, I felt as if I wanted to cry. As she bounded along, her long golden hair moving in the wind, I strained to capture the beguiling expression on her face and the mysterious suggestion in her eyes. Twice, she turned to face me, and when she did her penetrating eyes made direct contact with mine.

While the girl unquestionably fascinated me, I reacted to her direct gaze with alarm. When her eyes met mine, I actually felt myself being drawn into the scene more as a participant than just an observer.

Much to my regret, and despite my efforts to keep the girl and the soldier within view, they soon moved behind the wall and out of my field of vision. I wanted to follow her, but my body seemed paralyzed. As I reluctantly returned my attention to the other men and women at their tasks, I realized that each of them possessed the same vibrant spirit as the girl in the blue cloak.

In fact, the entire mountaintop fortress now seemed permeated with a palpable vitality. While I could see no statues, icons or altars, I began to sense that I was in a sacred place, and that these were holy people with a mission.

As I struggled to understand all that was happening to me, the peaceful atmosphere of Montségur suddenly erupted into chaos. The thunder of horses' hooves furiously pounding upon dry earth shattered the calm, and to my amazement I found myself gasping for breath, filled with a terrifying sense of panic.

The gentle people, who moments before had been quietly going about their work, began to scatter. Dogs barked angrily, huge stones began raining down from the sky, and the metallic clang of clashing swords rang through the air. What had felt like an enchanted dream had, in an instant, disintegrated into a nightmare!

What's happening? I wondered, my heart racing. What terrible force is assailing this place?

Then, just as suddenly as it had begun, the fury ceased. In the strange silence that followed, I somehow understood that by a twist of fate, the gentle people I had been observing had become the victims of an inexplicable force bent on their annihilation. I also knew that, despite its impressive structure, the mighty château of Montségur had failed to protect them.

Then, a heavy darkness settled upon the mountain, and I had the sense that terms of surrender had been arranged. At first I was relieved, expecting that the girl and the soldier and all the gentle people around them would now be safe from their oppressors.

However, I soon realized that whatever the terms of the negotiated surrender, peace would not follow. Now, I saw the residents of Montségur huddle close together, holding hands and speaking in muffled voices. Some walked in pairs along the wall of the mighty château, and for a moment I caught a glimpse of the young girl in the blue cloak. She was once again with the soldier, but now they sat together on a stone terrace, their faces wet with tears.

Once again, the girl looked directly at me, only this time her eyes seemed to be asking for something. What can she possibly want from me, I wondered?

My attention was suddenly drawn away from her by a disturbance along the outside wall. At first, I was unable to determine what was happening. But then, through the dim light, I saw three men being secured onto ropes and lowered silently down the sheer cliff on the steepest side of the mountain. The men appeared to be struggling with something they were carrying. Where were they going? And what were they taking away from Montségur ?

The deep despair written on their faces and the somber expressions of those assisting in their escape told me that these people would, in all likelihood, never see each other again. As I watched, their despair became my own, I felt tears well up and a sob form in my throat. Never had I felt so profoundly and hopelessly sad.

More than anything, however, I had a strong desire to get away from this place. But I didn't know how to wake myself from this terrible dream. As the darkness swallowed up the escaping men, a deafening silence settled on Montségur.

Then, a strange intermingling of incoherent sounds began to echo off the enormous walls. A sharp smell of smoke drifted into my nostrils, bearing a scent I couldn't quite identify. I watched, uncomprehending, as the gentle people of Montségur, in barefoot procession, started moving out through the castle's gate and down its sinuous path.

Are they being taken prisoner? I wondered. Are they being taken away from Montségur? No one seemed to resist, nor did they appear to be defeated.

As I frantically searched the scene, struggling to understand, I found the soldier, now crumpled on his knees. With eyes red and swollen, he watched as the young girl, her blue cloak wrapped tightly around her, moved past him, keeping pace with the others. In desperation, he called out to her repeatedly. I watched as she turned and smiled tenderly at him, looked at me once more, and then walked on.

Why was she leaving him? Where was she going? Why was he not going with her? The next thing I knew, I was listening to the wails of agonizing pain. They were unlike anything I'd ever heard before, and unable to bear listening further, I covered my ears. Only slowly did I recognize the horrifying smell in the air as that of burning flesh. Then, seconds later, I knew that the huge, hungry flames of an immense fire had consumed every one of them.

As a soul-numbing silence descended, a sudden gust of strong wind momentarily scattered the thick black cloud of smoke at the base of the mountain. I thought for a second I'd seen movement. Maybe, I prayed, the young girl with the penetrating eyes, or at least some of the others, had survived. Through the smoky haze I was able to distinguish a small group of black-robed men huddled together at the edge of the enormous fire. One of the men held a crucifix in his outstretched arm.

No longer able to watch the horror, I closed my eyes tightly.

When I opened them again, the entire scene had vanished. Once again I could feel the warm comfort of the sun on my skin and the fresh dampness of the earth beneath me. I felt disconnected from reality, and for a moment, I had no idea where I was.

Looking around, I remembered that I was alone at the Cathar château of Montségur. What in the world had happened to me? I was covered in sweat, my hands were dirty, and my clothes were rumpled. My body felt achy all over, as if I had been bruised. My eyes were burning.

I couldn't simply have fallen asleep. Had I tripped and hit my head? Had I lost consciousness? Had I somehow slipped into another dimension, another time, another reality? I had no answers. Nothing like this had ever happened to me before.

I wondered how much time had passed since I had first arrived at the summit of the mountain. My experience might have lasted hours, or it could have only been minutes. I looked at my wrist and discovered that I had forgotten to wear my watch.

As I sat up, a pair of French Air Force fighter jets flew by overhead, confirming in no uncertain terms that whatever had happened was over, and that I was back in contemporary time.

I tried to stand up, but was too shaky, and I hesitated before I tried again. All I wanted was to go home. I wanted to be in my car. I wanted to leave this place. I forced myself to stand up and begin walking down the mountain.

However, unlike my carefree climb up the mountain, my emotions were now in turmoil. When I finally began my descent along the rocky path, I felt shaky and uncertain, indescribably sad and deeply confused. I continued to ask myself, What on earth did I just see? And why?

As I stumbled along, my chaotic thoughts were unexpectedly interrupted by a pronounced rustle in the foliage that bordered the path leading down the mountain. Although I tried to ignore whatever I was hearing, it seemed to grow louder. My attention finally captured, I bent down and separated the greenery, thinking that an injured bird must be trapped.

Once I had moved aside the dense underbrush, I saw two large, brilliantly colored, sleek-bodied salamanders gazing straight up at me. Looking down at the four eyes staring back up at me gave me the oddest sensation. At first I wanted to laugh, but I didn't.

Why aren't these salamanders afraid of me? I marveled. Why are they just staring at me? And what am I doing on the side of a mountain, alone in the south of France, after having had the strangest experience of my entire life, locked in a staring match with a pair of salamanders?

As odd as it seemed, I had the distinct feeling that they were trying to tell me something. Then, I remembered that in mythology, salamanders were believed to be able to move through fire without being consumed by it. What a strange coincidence! I also knew that salamanders were used by many cultures to symbolize deep, personal transformation.

The salamanders' concentration remained fixed on me, and mine on them, for several minutes. I'd never seen wildlife behave like this before. Then, it occurred to me that since my visit to the haunted mountain top (for that was how I was beginning to think of it), I no longer had the right to expect that anything would ever again behave as I expected. With the four bright beady eyes continuing to gaze at me, I stood up and allowed the greenery to slowly fall back into place. By the time I finally got home that day, I was both exhausted and terribly disturbed.

"Did you get lost today?" Bill asked when I picked him up at work, "You look a little… I don't know exactly, upset?"

Much as I wanted to, I couldn't even begin to describe my experience. I just wanted to go to sleep. "Do you mind if we talk about it tomorrow?" I asked. He gave me a searching look, then kissed me on the forehead.

As I lay awake later that night, gazing out through the French doors leading from my bedroom to the garden, I reflected on what an extraordinary day it had been. There was no doubt in my mind—I was irrevocably changed, transformed. I felt as if I had unwillingly been drawn into a relationship with forces of which I had absolutely no understanding.

Maybe I really had tripped and bumped my head, I considered. Maybe it had all been just a dream, But then again, what kind of dream could have left me feeling as if I'd actually participated in such tragic events? And where exactly had the dream ended? Was it before or after my encounter with the salamanders?

One thing I knew for certain—I needed to find out about the Cathar: who they were, and what had happened to them up there on that mountain.

CHAPTER THREE

Music on the Green Hill

There are levels of reality far too mysterious for common sense.

Lyall Watson, *The Gifts of Unknown Things*

IN THE DAYS THAT FOLLOWED my visit to Montségur, I felt my center of gravity shift completely. My life, which had already been unsettled from the move to France, turned entirely upside down. Feeling anxious and empty, I could no longer concentrate on my reading and put *Les Misérables* aside, unfinished.

Now, all other thoughts had been replaced by one compelling notion: to learn who the Cathar were, and discover what had happened to them on that mountain. Nothing else seemed to matter. But how and where should I begin?

A few days later, while looking through the books at a local *tabac*, a bright blue, touristy-looking book called *Cathar Country*, with an aerial photograph of Montségur, caught my eye. Feeling a strange sense of exhilaration when I picked it up, I was relieved and excited to see that it was written in English.

I paid the clerk twenty *francs* and hurried home, the precious book in my hands. For the first time in weeks, my mind felt focused and clear, and I believed that my questions about Montségur and all that had happened to me would soon be answered.

Once home, I immediately opened the book to the index and searched for Montségur. Turning to the indicated page, I found a dazzling picture of the sheer pinnacle of limestone rock, the ruins of the haunted château perched at its crown. I shivered, but even more unsettling was reading the text and finding that the historic events it described at Montségur correlated exactly to what I had experienced there!

Apparently, back in the year 1229, most of the Cathar leaders had taken refuge behind Montségur's immense, unassailable walls. Refuge against whom? I wondered, but read on. For several years, under the protection of local knights, as many as 500 people had lived peacefully behind the walls of the château. Others had lived in surrounding huts built on the steep terraces at the foot of the castle's walls.

The residents of Montségur had lived for several years in relative safety. But the local population in the immediate area who provided supplies to those living on the mountain was continually terrorized by the soldiers of the Catholic Church. On thirty separate occasions, residents of the nearby town of Avignonet had been found guilty of heresy and sentenced to die at the stake.

This, I thought, was beginning to sound like the Inquisition, which I believed had taken place much later, and in Spain, not in France. As I read on, I learned that in 1242, after a particularly large burning in Avignonet, a band of dispossessed Southern lords and their knights, assisted by the enraged citizens of the town, rose up against their tormenters. They proceeded to murder two local representatives of the Catholic Church. This, apparently, was exactly the provocation the Church had been waiting for. In direct response, the Pope ordered that the fortress of Montségur, known to the Papal authorities as the *Vatican of the heresy*, be razed.

Could this be my own Catholic Church, in whose beliefs and traditions I had been steeped since childhood? Brushing these thoughts aside, I read on.

The crusaders who actually laid siege to Montségur numbered between 6,000 to 10,000 men, and had even included the Bishop of Albi, described as *a renowned engineer of heavy weaponry*. This was a strange and unholy vocation for a bishop, I thought.

I was also surprised to see the term, "Crusaders," mentioned. Weren't the Crusaders men who had fought in the Holy Lands against the infidels?

And where were all these soldiers coming from? More important, why were they persecuting the Cathar?

For ten long months, I learned, the Crusaders' strategy was to encircle Montségur and cut off the food supply from the valley. Their efforts, however, had failed. Sympathetic locals at considerable risk had secretly carried provisions up the mountain to their besieged neighbors.

Then, one dark, snowy night, a small band of Crusaders managed to sneak up the face of the northeast side of the mountain and set up a giant catapult. Cleverly designed by the Bishop of Albi, the catapult had been carried up the mountainside in pieces, assembled and then rained huge, deadly stones down upon the castle.

While the Cathar and their defenders huddled together and tended to their injuries, the Crusaders entered Montségur with swords drawn. I shuttered as I realized that what I was reading followed exactly what I had experienced!

Finally, exhausted and defeated, Montségur had surrendered and a fifteen-day truce between the Cathar leadership and the Crusaders was then arranged. According to the blue book, no one knows what exactly took place on the mountain during that time. One legend maintains that on the darkest night, three or four men slipped away down the side of the mountain carrying a Cathar treasure said to be of *inestimable value*. This was, I realized, probably the box I'd seen being spirited off the mountain.

The story continued. Apparently, at dawn on March 16th, 1244, an enormous fire had been built in a meadow at the foot of the mountain. As the flames had crackled in the early spring air, local noblemen and noblewomen, peasants, merchants, soldiers and husbands and wives, holding hands, had marched into the enormous fire.

This reminded me of the stories we'd been told from childhood of the Christians who'd been martyred by the Romans in the early days of the Christian Era. The nuns had taught us the tragic chronicles of these gentle and courageous martyrs and my missal had been laced with plastic-covered holy cards of these saints. I remembered that I'd been in awe of the courage of these people, and their plight had strengthened my faith in Christianity.

But now, it appeared, that these very gentle Christians were the ones who had brutally martyred the Cathar which ran to counter to everything I had ever been taught.

My head was swimming with questions. Why had I never learned anything about the Church waging a crusade in France against a heretic group called the Cathar? What kind of Pope could have been involved in the burning of almost 250 people? To my amazement, I learned that the name of the man responsible was, ironically, Pope Innocent the Third!

I looked down at my book again and began to page through it. I found pictures of St. Dominic and St. Bernard, both of whom were familiar to me. However I had no idea what their connection could have been with this slaughter.

Later that night, hoping to discover what could have turned the Church so violently against the Cathar, I read on. But nothing I read answered my questions. The blue book referred to the Cathar interchangeably as the *Albigensians, the Weavers, the Friends of God, the Good Men and Good Women,* and the *Bons Hommes* and *Bonnes Dames.* Sometimes, the Cathar seemed to be ordinary Christians who just didn't want to go to Church on Sunday or pay their tithes. But at other times, they were described as *Dualists, Manicheans, Arians, Gnostics* and *Bogomils,* terms I had never heard before and while they did not sound good, I had no idea what they meant.

Part of the problem was that what remained of the medieval Cathar story seemed a morass of legend, myth and historical fact. From what I could determine, almost every original Cathar document had been destroyed. What had been preserved were the Inquisition's own archives, which charged all its victims with the same crime, heresy.

To make matters even worse, I had very little understanding of medieval European history. The events concerning the massacre at Montségur had transpired in a place and at a time that I knew virtually nothing about.

What was very clear, however, was the powerful connection I felt to these medieval people. Since my experience at Montségur, I continued to see images of the beautiful young girl with her desperate look of appeal. Despite how confusing the story was, I felt more determined than ever to understand what exactly had happened to these people.

While the rest of the house slept, I continued my reading, slowly. This time, I learned that while the Cathar occupied the château at Montségur, the South of France hadn't been France at all, but a separate country called Occitania.

Reading on, I learned that during the Middle Ages, Occitania had been a prominent political, economic and cultural center of Europe. The rich, fertile land, described in the blue book as "a place where the sun always shone," had supported a graceful, sophisticated, and highly creative culture.

The medieval citizens of Occitania were patrons of the arts and literature. They honored diversity, aspired to social equality; women shared many rights with men, and championed ideas such as individualism and democracy. Its prosperous citizens had been well educated, fiercely independent and had spoken their own language, called "Occitan."

Occitan, I learned, had been the language of the legendary traveling minstrel/poets known as *troubadours*. Dante, the 16th century Florentine poet, had apparently contemplated using Occitan to compose his *Divine Comedy*, as he considered it the language most worthy of poetry. I wondered why I had never heard of this language or this place before.

From its description in the blue book, I was able to locate on our *Michelin* map where Occitania had once been. It rested below the Loire River, above the Pyrénées Mountains, and between the Mediterranean Sea and the Atlantic Ocean.

Having found it on the map, I realized that the same land today is called the Languedoc. Of course! I suddenly realized—Languedoc was the language, *langue*, of Occitan, the *langue de Oc*.

Some time between the twelfth and thirteenth century, the blue book reported, an idea called Catharism had appeared in Occitania. It was unclear whether the Cathar faith had been a new philosophy, or a concept whose origins were in antiquity. What was clear was that unlike the many Christian reform movements that had preceded it, the Cathar faith had taken root and flourished amongst the peace-loving citizens of Occitania.

My fascinating blue book contained beautiful photographs of over twenty Cathar châteaux, with a map showing their locations. Discouraged by all the questions it had failed to answer, I decided to use the blue book's map of the Cathar châteaux to see what I could find out first-hand, and resolved to continue my explorations.

Two days later, I set out alone on the *autoroute*, heading south. This time I decided to visit the castle of Puivert. For some reason, I was drawn to its picture in the book. It was also fairly close to Montségur, which seemed to be drawing me back to it.

On my way south, I stopped briefly in the hilltop town of Mirepoix, which according to my book had featured prominently in Cathar history. Evidently, many of the Cathar had lived in the town, and one of the town's nobles had played a key role in defending Montségur.

Now, as I wandered through the square with its beautiful arcades supporting medieval residences, I marveled at the wooden beams sculpted with heads of humans and monstrous animals.

When I entered one of the shops, I discovered another tourist book dedicated to the Cathar. This one was simply called, *The Cathar*. It was yellow and bore a British flag in the upper right hand corner, identifying it as an English translation. Delighted, I bought it without even opening it.

I then returned to my car and drove on towards Puivert. As I turned a bend in the road, a bleached stone castle rose up before me on the horizon. In contrast to Montségur's fearsome height and sheer rock walls, the rise of Puivert's green hill was gentle and inviting. Also, unlike Montségur, which lies mostly in ruin, what remained of Puivert was a picture-book fantasy of a medieval castle. From the road I could see a fortified wall with circular towers, a gatehouse with a dramatic arched entryway and a spectacularly tall, imposing rectangular tower that dominated the entire structure.

It was obvious that Puivert had once been a place of great prominence and grace. Where Montségur had felt like a fortress sanctuary in the sky, Puivert felt like a lovely hillside manor.

After parking my car in the empty parking lot, I got out and, with my new yellow book in hand, sat down on the ground to read the description of the castle. In 1107, following the wedding of Eleanor of Aquitaine's daughter in the castle's chapel, a large gathering of *troubadours* had been held here.

How exciting! Eleanor of Aquitaine had actually been here. As I recalled, she had been married to a French king, and was the mother of Richard the Lionheart.

When I realized that such a renowned medieval woman had actually been on these grounds, I was filled with awe. And what an absolutely perfect place for a wedding! According to my yellow book, which seemed considerably more informative than my blue book, an Occitan poet who documented the event said he composed his verse "to the sound of bagpipes, among songs and laughter."

Looking up at charming Puivert, or *The Green Hill,* and seeing the summer breezes gently waving the tall grasses circling its bleached stone walls, I could imagine the merrymaking that had taken place here. More than Montségur, this graceful château exemplified what I imagined life in medieval Occitania to have been.

But while the castle brought images of music and gaiety to mind, the yellow book revealed that it had also experienced tremendous tragedy during the Church's crusade against the Cathar.

There it was again, that word, crusade. While it took no effort to imagine a wedding here, the thought of a crusade at this peaceful castle was almost inconceivable. It was far too lovely to have been the scene of war.

But I was wrong. Puivert, from what I read, had been taken following a bloody three-day siege and was awarded as booty to Simon de Montfort, the highest-ranking knight of the crusade.

According to the yellow book, the Lord of Puivert, an unwavering supporter of the Cathar, had died at the château Montségur, and his young daughter had been burned there in the great fire of 1244.

I shuddered at the thought. Then standing-up, I closed the book and found my way to the footpath leading up to the castle, a poorly defined trail through the tall field grasses and wildflowers. As I approached the gate to the castle, a profound sense of wonder came over me. But once through the arched entry of the gatehouse and between the castle walls, I suddenly became frightened.

I stopped moving and looked around, but there was no one to be seen; Puivert appeared to be completely empty. There was no sound other than the light rustling of the ivy on the castle walls. Yet, despite the silence, I felt a presence, as if within the stillness someone or something was alive and alert. It felt oddly as if I had walked into a room and awakened someone or something that had been sleeping.

I found myself wondering, Are these Cathar châteaux really haunted? If so, both my guidebooks seem to have omitted that vital piece of information.

I didn't want to go through anything resembling what I had experienced at Montségur, and considered turning back. But curiosity led me forward. Oh, come on, I reassured myself. There's no one here and you're not going to fall asleep or trip and lose consciousness again. It would be silly to have come all this way and not see the place.

Buoyed by my new resolve, I headed toward the huge rectangular tower, which I suspected was the *keep*, the living quarters of the castle's inhabitants. I noticed that as I walked across the open courtyard, my fear began to subside. Now, I began to visualize medieval pageantry and tournaments in progress. It was easy to envision armored knights jousting on their noble steeds, their colorful banners waving on the wind in this courtyard. I could almost hear music.

As I approached the keep, I found an outside staircase that appeared to lead to an entryway. Gripping a rusted metal hand rail, an obvious signature of modern times, I climbed up and into the structure.

The tower was three stories high. Each story, I learned from the yellow book, had been used by the resident noble family for a different purpose. On the first floor, which the yellow book identified as the guardroom, I found another stone staircase, which I climbed to the top floor.

I needed no book to tell me that the room at the top of the tower had been Puivert's crown jewel. The Great Hall, or as the book described it, the *Musician's Chamber* or *Minstrel's Hall*, was absolutely magnificent. The yellowing stone corbels at the base of the ribbed vaulted ceiling arches were decorated with carvings of eight medieval musicians holding their musical instruments.

Three of the instruments were unfamiliar to me. However, I could identify among the others a bagpipe, a lute, a violin of some sort, a small handheld drum, and a woodwind or reed instrument.

There was no hint here of heretics or crusades, no sadness or suggestion of smoke—in short, there was nothing to indicate that a tragedy had ever befallen Puivert.

From the *Musician's Chamber*, I descended the staircase to the second, or middle, level of the keep, heading for the chapel. This room was also very beautiful, lit by two large arched windows that provided fantastic vistas of the surrounding plain.

Richly woven tapestries of red and gold adorned the walls—or did I just imagine that? On my way across the room to admire the gothic windows, I listened closely, hearing once again what sounded like music. As I strained to locate its source, I suddenly felt dizzy and instinctively headed toward the window casing to sit down.

As soon as I did, I immediately felt better. Looking out the window, for as far as I could see, was an unbroken vista of softly rolling fields kissed by a sky of porcelain blue. The lovely view settled me and my dizziness passed. A warm breeze drifted through the window, brushed against my cheek and rustled my hair.

I should have brought a bottle of water from the car, I thought, suddenly feeling very thirsty. Wait! Had I just heard music again? I whirled around to see. But there was nothing to account for what I thought I heard. When I turned back around to face the open window, fully awake and conscious, I found the scene completely changed.

Moments before, there had been only fields. Now I was looking at a medieval dreamscape of Puivert. The strange events that had befallen me at Montségur, despite all my efforts to prevent them, were once again taking hold of me! Unable to resist the compulsion to look outside, I peered through the castle window and could see a group of gentlemen on horseback at the base of the hill.

They were all young and handsome, dressed in tunics of rich, forest green, indigo and crimson. And they seemed to be waiting for something. Their metal belts shone in the sunlight, and I could almost smell the fine polished leather of their high boots. The horses wore saddlebags, clearly prepared for a journey. They shrugged, twitched their tails and pawed the ground as if anxious to leave.

While all in the group appeared to be close friends, one man was obviously the leader. He rode a beautiful, cream-colored horse and wore a tunic of finely woven linen. I watched him speak with an air of authority that reflected both confidence and respect for his colleagues.

His face was quite handsome. He had a rugged complexion, a proud patrician nose, a gentle mouth with a bottom lip that tucked slightly beneath the top and sandy brown hair. His eyes spoke of the summer and the sea and of the bleached stones of Occitania. I could hear the faint tinkling sound of his horse's bridle as he moved amongst the group, talking and laughing with his friends.

I was surprised when suddenly I caught sight of a young girl running down the path toward them. She was wearing a light blue silken dress and her unbound golden hair blew behind her as she hurried along the gentle slope of Puivert's hill. As she approached the men, she headed directly for the leader of the group. When she came up alongside him, her face lit up with a joy so intense I could actually feel it.

The man reached down with one arm and pulled her easily up into his saddle. I marveled at the way I was feeling, just watching them. He buried his face in her hair and seemed to be whispering into her ear. Then she turned to face him and kissed him tenderly on the mouth. After a long embrace with both his hands around her small waist, he lowered her to the ground.

It was clear that all the others had been waiting for her to arrive so their leader could say his goodbyes to her, and she to him. As the girl backed away so the horses could pass, her lover raised a gloved hand to his lips and blew her a final kiss. Then along with the others, he rode away.

I somehow knew that his ride would bring him to a battle he would not wish to fight, to a crusade he would wish to have no part in. I knew that his days of sleeping beneath an Occitan moon and rising to the warmth of an Occitan sun were numbered. I knew he would not return to the land, or to the girl, that he loved so dearly.

I watched the colors of the riders and their horses slowly fade into the landscape. From time to time, the man looked back at his beloved. I watched and listened as their departing sounds soon became silence.

My attention had been so fixed on the men as they rode away that I nearly forgot about the girl. When I looked for her, I found her standing where I had last seen her. As she slowly turned away from the emptiness in the distance, she looked up to the castle window and her eyes met mine. I recognized her immediately.

She was the girl I had seen at Montségur, and again, she looked at me with the same appealing expression she had sent me earlier.

And then, she was gone. When I could see only emptiness beneath the vastness of the sky, a deep sense of loneliness overcame me. Tears burned in my eyes, but I didn't let them fall, frightened that if I did, the powerful feelings rising within me would totally overwhelm me. As I turned my gaze back into the chapel, I was left with feelings of deep loneliness and profound grief.

The drive home seemed endless. I'm not even sure how I found my way. Back in the house I checked the clock and saw that I had about an hour before my kids came home. I dropped into bed and slept soundly, only to awaken when I heard tired and hungry voices in the kitchen.

I jumped up, barely awake, to welcome Rachel and Nicholas back home, giving them long hugs and telling them how very glad I was to see them. They both looked at each other and rolled their eyes.

"Mom!" said Nicholas, pulling away from me. "I'm happy you're glad to see us, but I'm starving!"

"All right, then," I said, "let's get you something to eat." I grabbed a *baguette*, the jar of *Nutella* and a bottle of juice, and then sat down to listen to my children tell me about the challenges they had faced that day at school. I was so very happy that we were all safe at home, together.

When they had finished their snacks, they went into the living room and turned on the TV. I could hear *Hélène et les Garçons* as I put the dishes into the sink. I wondered what they would think if I told them what had happened to me today. How could I ever explain these experiences to anyone? Who would understand? Surely they would think I'd lost my mind... and maybe in fact, I had.

CHAPTER FOUR

The Pierced Rock

What is hidden always prevails over what is seen.

Stephan Hoeller, *The Gnostic Jung*

AFTER DINNER, I HELPED THE KIDS with their homework. Once they had gone to bed, I curled up with Bill on the living room couch and we watched TV together. It felt amazingly normal, and therefore, amazingly good. A part of me wished desperately that I could just return to the simplicity of what my life had been before my visit to "the haunted châteaux." But it was, I sensed, too late for "normalcy."

That night, I dreamed of the girl from Montségur, whom I had seen again at Puivert. This time, she was running and I was following close behind. Although we ran and ran, we never seemed to get anywhere. The girl was always in front of me, turning around from time to time to beckon me on, but wherever we were going, we never arrived. When I awoke the next morning, I was exhausted.

A few days later, on a beautiful Saturday afternoon, Bill suggested that we take a drive into Cathar country. I hesitated, not sure I really wanted to go. But this was Bill's first chance to see it, and he enticed me to join him.

"Come on, it's a beautiful day. We can take a picnic," he urged.

That night, the kids would be staying with friends, and it did seem like the perfect opportunity for us to explore the area together.

"Besides," pressed Bill, "I think it's time I got a firsthand look at this new interest of yours, these Cathar."

I'd been talking to Bill whenever I'd gotten a chance, sharing all that I'd been reading in my blue and yellow books. Finally, I agreed to go, and this time I selected the castle at Arques as our destination. According to the blue book's map, it was only a bit farther from Toulouse than Montségur, perhaps an hour's drive.

While Bill changed his clothes, I put together a picnic from what I could find in the kitchen: some cheese, a few olives, a tin of sardines, a bunch of cherry tomatoes, and the remains of the *baguette* from lunch. Then, I charted our course on the *Michelin* map.

As Bill drove, I read aloud from my new yellow Cathar book. During the 12th and 13th centuries, the village of Arques had been home to a large population of Cathar heretics. Later, in the 20th century, it had been home to a man named Déodat Roché, who was very important to the Cathar.

Roché, according to the book, had almost single-handedly led the effort to lift the pall of silence that for centuries had hung over the story of the Cathar. Until his research and that of those who followed in his footsteps, like René Nelli and Jean Duvernoy, the entire history of these people and the terrible crusade waged against Occitania had been virtually removed from the pages of history.

"That's incredible," said Bill. "It's hard to believe that an entire culture could be just wiped off the map with no one left to tell the story."

"Listen to this," I said. "According to my book, the Cathar faith was somehow connected to Mithraism, a popular ancient religion in the Roman Empire right before the rise of Christianity. Its founder was named Mithra. And do you want to hear the most amazing coincidence?"

"Ok, what's the coincidence?" Bill asked, playing along.

"Mithra's birthday was on December 25th, the same day as Jesus'. Don't you think that's curious, that another founder of a religion from the same part of the world had the same birthday as Jesus?"

Bill had also been raised Catholic. And while he'd never gone to Catholic school and hadn't been nearly as involved with the Church as I'd been, this bit of information was as surprising to him as it had been to me.

"That is an awfully odd coincidence," he agreed.

As we pulled off the highway and left behind the sounds of its speeding cars, the air fell silent. Cathar country emitted an amazing silence; I'd experienced it each time I'd come here and the timeless, elemental quiet seemed to stir something deep inside me.

I closed the book and placed it on the back seat. Surrounding us on every side were endless fields of grapevines with no other signs of life, until we came to the town of Limoux.

I had read about this town, and told Bill, "This place is famous for its bubbling white wine called *blanquette*. It's like champagne, but it was discovered centuries before the monk, Dom Perignon, in the north of France, purportedly stumbled on the process."

Signs along the road promoted *blanquette* as well as a local candy called *nougat*. Once outside Limoux, everything became perfectly quiet again. The road narrowed and wound around until eventually we came to a sign that said, ARQUES.

We turned left and minutes later entered the village, which seemed to have drifted off to sleep centuries earlier. Its castle, far lovelier than the photographs in either of my books suggested, looked as if someone had simply blown out the candles and gone away.

Unlike both Montségur and Puivert, Arques stood at ground level. Despite being what the yellow book described as "a masterpiece of military architecture," its four towers looked surprisingly delicate and feminine, almost as if a woman had been responsible for their design.

As we walked through the castle gate decorated with a coat of arms, we saw no signs of life. Arques sat, as did Puivert and Montségur, silent and frozen in time. We headed through the yard toward a large square keep flanked at each corner by a tower.

Bill took my hand. "Let's check out one of the towers," he said. As we entered and began the climb up the narrow, twisting stone staircase, he pointed down at each stair. "Those look like some kind of animal droppings, but they're too large to be from mice or rats. And what would mice be doing in here, anyway? It doesn't look as if there's been any food around here for several hundred years."

Perplexed, we continued our climb and soon reached the top. The narrow, circular room at the summit of the staircase had probably been the noble family's living quarters.

Suddenly, as I looked up into the apex of the tower, I gasped. Something was moving. Actually, the entire top of the tower was moving, pulsating and breathing!

"Oh, my God!" said Bill, grabbing my hands and pulling me back down the stairs. "It's bats!" His deep voice had startled the creatures awake, and now they were dropping from the ceiling and flying toward us. We ran down the stairs much faster than we had ascended them, and seconds later were outside in the castle yard.

After catching our breath and making sure that none of the bats was following us, we explored more of the castle. This time, we proceeded a bit more cautiously, looking up to the ceiling before entering any other rooms. While I was certainly no fan of bats, in some ways the little winged creatures seemed less frightening than the ghostly experiences I had encountered at the other Cathar châteaux.

When we tired of our explorations, we decided to set up our picnic. Bill walked back to the car for the basket and I found a spot outside the gate to spread our blanket.

For the next hour or so we sat in the tall, wild grasses in front of Arques, feasting on our picnic. When we finished, we both lay down on the blanket, and as I looked up at the castle towers, my mind began to drift.

After awhile I completely forgot where I was and let myself waft in and out of a series of odd, disconnected images. They involved things I couldn't quite place: a very dry colorless landscape, a tunnel cut into a rocky mountain, a particularly beautiful sky above a flowering orchard, and the melodic sound of a woman's voice.

As the afternoon began to wane, Bill broke the silence. "We should probably be starting home, don't you think?"

I didn't want to leave, but agreed anyway. This was the first time I had visited a Cathar château and not seen the girl. I was relieved, but at the same time I oddly felt a little sad. Was it, I wondered, because I was here with someone else?

Once packed up and back in the car, we headed for home. But right beyond the village of Arques I saw a sign for PEYREPERTUSE, with an arrow pointing to the left. It was the kind of sign that implies that the destination it is pointing to is very close by.

"That's the name of another Cathar château," I said. "It means 'Pierced Rock.'"

"Really?" replied Bill? "Do you want to see it?" To my surprise, without waiting for my answer, he made the turn.

"OK," I replied, a bit taken aback by his enthusiasm. As time passed, however, both of us became uneasy when we realized that the sign had been deceptive. The château was hardly around the corner; in fact, it proved to be quite a distance away. As we drove on and on, we began to ask each other whether we had made the wrong decision. Maybe we just should have gone home.

Now, there were no towns or villages in sight and no other cars. As we continued deeper and deeper into the Pyrénées, we became more and more tense. Maybe we had missed a turn. Maybe we had missed another sign. Worst of all, the sun was beginning to slip down towards the horizon.

"I'm almost sure we're heading towards the sea," said Bill. "But I feel as if we're being swallowed up by the mountains."

Just then, something caught my eye in the distance. It looked for a moment like a castle wall. Or was it just rock?

"It's a natural rock formation," said Bill when I pointed it out to him. "But wait a minute, maybe not." As we got closer, the rock seemed more defined, more like something that had been shaped by human hands.

Soon we realized that we had reached our destination. We were looking at the enormous walls of Peyrepertuse merging seamlessly with a huge natural pinnacle of rock. From a distance, the castle looked totally inaccessible, and as we got closer, I was sure that the climb to the top would take hours.

When we finally arrived at its base and found the overgrown path to its entryway, I hesitated. "It's getting dark," I said. "Maybe we should come back another time. We might make it up before the sun sets, but what about getting down?"

But Bill jumped from the car, eager to explore. I followed and he came around, grabbed my hand, and said, "Let's go!"

We began to run up the path, following its winding route around the steep sides of the mountain, moving higher and higher. In the daylight this would be a difficult climb, I told myself. What will happen when it gets dark?

We reached the top just as the setting sun met the castle walls. Brilliant rays of golden light shot across the stone and illuminated the interior of the roofless structure. The warm, golden glow made me forget momentarily that I was thousands of feet in the air and that it would soon be dark.

The castle was extraordinary. It crowned the earth and touched the heavens. Standing inside its walls I felt a sense of real exhilaration, and was glad we'd come.

The views in every direction were awesome. "This outer wall must be a mile long! There's the Mediterranean!" said Bill, pointing to the distant turquoise water shimmering in the fading light. We could also see the soaring silver walls of another castle dominating a not too distant peak.

Suddenly, I felt a sense of impending danger as a gust of wind lifted my sweater off my shoulder and tossed it several feet in front of me. I had the feeling that we should reconsider going any farther. For some reason, I no longer felt safe.

Bill must have felt something uncomfortable, as well. "Let's hurry," he said. I picked up my sweater and followed behind him. Inside the enormous rock walls, the castle revealed astoundingly beautiful features; majestic towers, arched windows, a beautiful staircase built over a sheer bluff, terraces with breathtaking vistas.

We hurried through the interior of the castle, only to halt before what was clearly the castle's chapel. A stone altar left no doubt of the significance of the room. As we stopped to explore, the light in the roofless enclosure suddenly turned an unearthly shade of violet. I gasped.

"It's the sun," said Bill, taking my hand. "It's only the light of the sun." But then, a stream of purple iridescent light shot through the arched windows of the chapel's walls and illuminated the altar with a strange glow. We stood speechless. It looked as if the light had intentionally been directed through the window and straight to the altar.

"We should go," said Bill abruptly, and to my surprise, I became aware for the first time that Bill was actually frightened. This only intensified my own fear.

I sensed that when Bill had searched his scientifically oriented mind for an explanation for the light and not found one, his internal alarm system had gone off. He took my hand again, and this time we began to run.

The château was massive beyond belief, and it would have taken hours to explore it fully. We arrived at the base of the mountain breathless and shaken by our memories of the extraordinary light in the chapel.

Back in the car again, we headed in the direction of the Mediterranean, away from Arques, away from Peyrepertuse and toward the sea, where we knew we would find the *autoroute* and our way home.

"I don't think I understand what's going on here," Bill began once we were in route. "These châteaux really do feel haunted. Tell me again, who exactly were these Cathar?"

"I don't really know," I replied. "I'm doing everything I can to find out, but I'm afraid I'm not making much progress. They believed, I think, that at the core of every human being is a *spark of light* that originated with God—a spark of light that's trying to find its way home."

"Speaking of light," Bill interrupted. "Did it seem to you as if that window had been designed to actually focus the sunlight directly on the altar? Do you think that's possible? Or was it just a strange coincidence?"

"I don't know," I replied, relieved to be back in the car and on our way home. "But doesn't the sun's position constantly shift with the time of day and the changes of season? It must have been a coincidence," I concluded. Bill agreed, and we drove along in silence, lost in our own thoughts.

After awhile, I turned on the interior light, reached into the back seat and pulled out my yellow Cathar book. I looked up Peyrepertuse in the index and turned to the page indicated. The name of the chapel with the amazing violet light, I learned, was St. Mary's. St. Mary, I wondered? I'd never heard of the Blessed Virgin Mary referred to as St. Mary. Who was St. Mary?

CHAPTER FIVE

Occitania, the Land of Secrets

> One has to trust the inner directives
> of the Quest whatever the cost, and often without knowing
> for a long time after if one really did choose wisely.
>
> John Matthews, *The Grail Quest*

BEFORE WE HAD EVEN LEFT THE STATES, my sister, Julie, and her husband, Toby had made plans to take their summer vacation in France with us. With their arrival now only days away I was forced to put aside my preoccupation with the heretic Cathar. There were at least a million things I needed to do before our home beneath the spires of the neighboring château would be ready to welcome company.

However, that afternoon, after purchasing new pillows and extra towels in downtown Toulouse, I couldn't resist stopping into a large bookstore at a corner of the *Place du Capitole.* On a table in the center of the store I came across a book in English on the history of the Catholic Church. The quote on the cover heralded it as an *up to date, concise history of the Church and a must for every teacher and librarian.*

While it was quite expensive, I bought it anyway, very curious as to what, if anything, it would say about the Cathar and the crusade against Occitania. I hurried home, and finding the kids engaged in a ping-pong match, decided to sneak a quick look. I was hardly prepared, however, for what followed.

The five-hundred-page book offered only a brief, one-page reference to the crusade. The fact that it had been delegated to a position of such insignificance in Church history was surprising enough, but what truly amazed me was that the author had depicted the medieval Church during the Occitan crusade as an institution fiercely committed to *morality, order and righteousness.* In his words, this rampage of death and punishment had been *the most stabilizing element in medieval society,* having *put the modern world very much in its debt.*

The author went on to offer high praise for Pope Innocent III, the instigator of the crusade against the Cathar, referring to him as one of the *greatest Popes in history.* His papacy was characterized as a remarkable success and he was praised for his courage in *crushing the heretics.* The crusade itself was referred to as his victory and triumph and Pope Innocent's need to resort to *different tactics* was commended.

How, I wondered, could anyone accept that all this savagery had been carried out by a moral, righteous institution—not to mention that the institution had supposedly been founded on the teachings of *the Prince of Peace?* And how was it possible to call burning people to death a *different tactic?*

Even more amazing was how the same organization that had acted so reprehensibly could today be considered a spiritual authority. This was the same Catholic Church that had claimed authority to teach me right from wrong, and offered me penance and forgiveness when I had confused the two. Surely what had happened in Occitania was as evil as anything I had ever encountered.

While growing up, I had certainly had my issues with the Church, but I had always trusted in its basic goodness. Now, that trust had been shaken, perhaps for good. A call from the kitchen interrupted my thoughts. "Mom! I'm hungry! When are we going to eat?" Nicholas pleaded.

Later that night, with dinner finished, the dishes done, and everyone engaged in their individual activities, I sat down at the table in the garden. It was a beautiful evening. A full moon was rising above the neighboring château. I could hear the sounds of my son, Nicholas, playing with his Lego through his open door. He had hundreds, maybe even thousands of colorful Lego blocks and had insisted that his entire collection accompany him to France. I had tried hard to convince him otherwise. But at this moment, I was very glad he had won the argument.

For some reason, I always found the sounds of Nicholas scooping up, and then dropping handfuls of the tiny plastic blocks into their bin, strangely calming. Tonight the sounds were particularly soothing. It gave me the sensation that despite all that was happening to suggest the contrary, life continued to go on around me as usual.

Two days later, my sister and her husband arrived. "We're here for some *joie de vivre*!" they announced as they threw their suitcases into the trunk of our car at the airport in Toulouse. It was wonderful to see them; now I had somebody from home with whom to share our world. My sister always made me laugh and I was really looking forward to some fun and relaxation.

Wary that my anger with the Church might be contagious and that my obsession with the Cathar might worry my sister and her husband, I resolved not to mention anything about my discovery of the medieval heretics and their fate; I was certain that, at the very least, it would darken their holiday mood.

But things did not go as planned. We spent the first day of their visit catching up on family news and basking in the warm sunshine. Then, on the second day, my sister picked up a book from my nightstand. "What's a Cathar?" she asked.

"Oh," I replied, snatching the book out of her hand. "Trust me; you really don't want to know. Put the book down and move away from it quickly. Just forget you ever saw it."

"Judging from that response," said Julie. "I really think I do need to know. Come on, let's hear it. What's a Cathar?"

"The Cathar were heretics," I said tersely. "Now are you satisfied?"

"Not really," she replied. "Are they heretics from France? From around here?"

She took the book back from me and started paging through it. " Wow, where are these places? These castles are beautiful! What do they have to do with the heretics?' Have you been to any of them? Are they close by? Look at this one," she exclaimed, turning the book around and showing me a picture. "I want to see it. Can we go?"

Thus ended my intentions to keep the Cathar and the Crusade against Occitania from my sister. In fact, Julie wanted to know everything she could about them, and over dinner she assailed me with questions. Her husband, Toby, was surprisingly interested as well.

"She's become totally obsessed with this," Bill told Toby as he poured him a glass of wine.

"She doesn't think about anything else," added Nicholas.

"Be careful, Aunt Julie," Rachel chimed in, "It could happen to you!"

"And we can't guarantee that there's any way back," laughed Bill.

"It's true," I admitted. "I can't explain it. I only know that I am profoundly compelled by these people and the history of this land."

"So are we going to see some of these castles Julie's been talking about?" asked Toby

After dinner, when Julie and I were alone, I told her about my experiences at Montségur and at Puivert.

"You just fell asleep at a tourist site?" asked Julie disbelievingly. "That doesn't sound like something you would do."

"I wasn't asleep," I insisted. "I actually don't know what happened to me. But I've corroborated almost everything I experienced at Montségur by reading all about the history of the place. And before I went there I didn't know a single thing about it."

"I want to go," Julie announced firmly. "Tomorrow, OK? We didn't come with an itinerary," she added, "but if you don't mind, we've got one now!"

So the next morning, and almost every day for the next two weeks, we rose early and sleepily set out to visit what, in 1203, Pope Innocent III had designated the *infected limb that must be cut off quickly before the whole body becomes infected.*

Every morning, along with Julie, Toby, Bill (who had taken time off from work), and occasionally our children, I packed the car with water, cameras, sweaters, my guidebooks and a map and we headed south into *le pays de Cathare* to learn first hand the story of the heretics.

Each day, as we climbed among the crumbling ruins of the Cathar châteaux, picnicked on the local breads and cheeses and drank the warm red wines of the Corbiéres, we found ourselves falling more and more deeply under the spell of the medieval land of Oc.

Maybe it was the quality of light that seduced us, or the gentleness of the winds, or the ruggedness of the land and the sparkling blue of the Mediterranean beyond the Pyrénées. Whatever it was, we were pulled completely into its raw beauty, its enduring hope, its profound sorrow and its irresistible whisper of mystery.

Intuition more than anything else guided our itinerary. Like beacons of light, the last vestiges of the medieval Cathar seemed to pull us toward them. Each town we visited, whether large or small, invited us to walk its streets, to taste its wine, to sit in its sunshine, and to hear its sad history.

We hadn't intended to visit the hilltop town of Fanjeaux, but a road sign pointing the way to the House of St. Dominic changed our plans. I remembered previously seeing the picture of the popular saint in my blue Cathar book. Interested in how the founder of the monastic order of Dominicans had been connected to the Cathar, we stopped to find out. After parking the car we followed the signs to *La Maison de Saint Dominique*.

Walking along the narrow streets of tiny Fanjeaux, past the honey-colored stone houses, their windows shuttered securely against the hot afternoon sun, it was hard to believe that the town had ever been more than a sleepy little hamlet. But according to our guidebook it had been a *hotbed of heresy*. It had also been home to the Spanish monk, Dominic Guzmán, who had been ordered to Occitania by Pope Innocent III to halt the alarming spread of the Cathar heresy.

Dominic, we learned, had been a pious monk committed to a life of simplicity. He was also an irresistible preacher with a proven track record for peacefully persuading heretics to return to the Church. In the early days of the thirteenth century, the local Catholic clergy were living extravagant and corrupt life styles, selling sacraments, ignoring the needs of their congregations, and failing miserably when trying to deal with the Cathar.

Dominic was the miracle the Church counted on. His successful strategy for reconciling lost souls to the *one true faith* was to organize large public debates where he could defend the superiority of Church doctrine against the heresy. But his prior experience with heretics had not prepared him for the Cathar. In previous situations, we learned, he had dealt with heretics who were illiterate and incapable of successfully challenging his expert theological explanations and spiritual arguments.

The Cathar, however, were not only literate, but many were highly educated and of noble birth. They were also well acquainted with the Bible, and thus highly qualified to defend themselves theologically. In fact, the Cathar not only preached from their own Bible when personal ownership of the Bible was prohibited—they had the audacity to have translated the book into Occitan!

Women presented yet another unexpected difficulty for Dominic. While the medieval Church considered women to be moral deviants and impediments to spirituality, Cathar women shared leadership equally with men. A record of one of Dominic's famous debates describes a *pious and beautiful* noblewoman and Cathar initiate, Esclarmonde de Foix, whose name in Occitan means *light of the world*. She apparently enraged one of Dominic's associates by participating in a public debate. Furious, the priest is said to have jumped to his feet and ordered Esclarmonde to return to her "spinning and woman's work."

The story of Esclarmonde fascinated us and we made a note to learn more about her.

Despite the challenges he faced, we learned that Dominic performed several astonishing miracles while residing in Fanjeaux. One miracle involved a field of bleeding corn. Another had to do with a fiery comet strangely falling from the sky.

The most famous of Dominic's miracles, chronicled by a representative of the Church, took place when the notes he had used at one of the debates were thrown into a fire to test their veracity. Amazing a crowd of onlookers, the notes flew up out of the fire and rose to the ceiling, completely undamaged by the flames. There is a charred beam hanging on chains in a chapel of the Fanjeaux cathedral that is said to be evidence of this trial by fire, and a painting at the Louvre by Fra Angelico illustrates the event.

In addition to his many miracles, during his time in Occitania, Dominic founded the monastic order of the Dominican Friars and started a convent for a small group of Cathar women he had inducted back into the Church. According to our guidebook, his convent was established in an ancient church dedicated to St. Mary.

There was that name again. Was it a mistake? Did it refer to the Blessed Mother?

While Dominic's accomplishments in Occitania were many, he failed to perform the one miracle the Church needed, the only miracle the Pope had counted on. His debates did not peacefully persuade the heretics to return to the Church; instead, the Cathar heresy had continued to grow.

When one of the Pope's emissaries was mysteriously murdered, the situation in Occitania took an abrupt turn for the worse. Further debates with the Cathar were halted, Dominic was called home and Pope Innocent III ordered that *Anyone attempting to construe a personal view of God which conflicts with Church dogma must be burned without pity.*

As we prepared to leave Fanjeaux, I paused for a moment before getting into the car. I looked back out across the wide Lauragais plain with its tidy fields of sunflowers, lavender and waves of ripening grapes and tried to imagine the debates that had taken place there.

According to our guidebook, hundreds, maybe thousands of spectators had set aside their looms, flocks, anvils and ovens to attend. Peasants, *troubadours*, knights and noblemen and women had stood side by side in these fields listening for words to lift them up and out of the doldrums of their daily lives and into the world of spirit.

I scanned the plain, looking for hints of movement, straining to hear whispers. But in this land of secrets, in this sun-drenched land of intense and mysterious beauty that never failed to move me, nothing stirred. There was only a cold silence.

In fact, the town of Fanjeaux seemed like a canvas that had been painted over. Dominic's home had been restored as a shrine, his church lavishly renovated and the convent he founded at Prouille was now an international community of Dominican nuns. Like my new book on Church history, in Fanjeaux there was barely a mention of the crusade. While the town had actually served as the headquarters for the crusaders, all that remained now was a sense of, "Let's forget about it and move on."

But none of us could do that. Even though seven centuries had passed, we were compelled for reasons none of us understood to learn everything we could about what had really happened here.

CHAPTER SIX

The Crusade Against the Cathar

The heretic is not he who burns in the flames,
but he who lights the stake.

William Shakespeare

AS WE TRAVELED on through Cathar country, we learned that in June, 1209, right after St. Dominic's failed mission, the Pope, proceeded to mount the first crusade, or Holy War, ever to be convened on Western soil against European Christians. The intention of the Church was to rid Christendom of all in the Southern lands that had *strayed dangerously from the one true path.*

In response to the Pope's call to crusade, we learned, knights, noblemen, and foot soldiers from the Northern French kingdom and beyond put aside their daily labors and gathered under the papal banner. They responded to the Pope's call to defend the Church, motivated by the offer of free southern land to anyone who could capture it, a guaranteed forgiveness of all previous and future sins, and an assured place in heaven. As many as 130,000 men rallied to defend the true faith.

The forces assembled by the Church included some of the most renowned nobles in the Northern French kingdom, as well as hordes of villainous thieves and criminals anxious to cash in on the Pope's bounty. Under the leadership of a monk named Arnaud Amaury, the Church's armies descended upon the peace-loving citizens of Occitania, whose nobles were poorly prepared for a military confrontation.

As we drove along the auto route toward the town of Béziers, my brother-in-law read from our guidebook. Young Raymond Robert Trencavel, we learned, was among the three most powerful Southern nobles. While well aware of the deteriorating situation between the Church and Occitania, he was shocked to learn that an enormous army had been assembled by the Pope and was marching toward his lands, specifically toward the town of Béziers.

Realizing the imminent threat and hoping to avoid a direct confrontation, Trencavel raced to Béziers to meet the approaching crusaders. His intention, in accordance with chivalric tradition, was to present himself to Arnaud Amaury and offer to reconcile with the Church.

Trencavel's offer however was flatly turned down and he was ordered instead to tell the citizens of Béziers to open the gates and hand over the town's 222 *notable heretics.*

"222?" I interrupted.

"That's what it says here," answered Toby and he read on. The citizens of Béziers, Toby continued, absolutely refused to comply with this order. Subsequently, the following afternoon, on July 22nd, *the Feast Day of Saint Mary Magdalene,* the Crusaders launched a surprise attack on the town. According to the story, while the battle lasted only one day, when it was over, every inhabitant of the town, including men, women, children, the elderly and the ill, whether Catholic or heretic, had been slaughtered.

The answer given to the crusaders who asked Arnaud Amaury, how they would distinguish the Christians in the town from the heretics, has continued to echo through the centuries, "Kill them all. God will recognize His own."

Among those massacred were the 6,000 who had taken refuge, along with their Catholic priest, in the town's cathedral of St. Mary Magdalene. In a letter written to Pope Innocent III on the afternoon of the attack, Arnaud Amaury reported that over 20,000 people in the city had been *put to the sword.*

"It's so hard to imagine," said Bill shaking his head as we sat together later beneath the shade of an ancient plane tree on the town square. "Every single person in the town slaughtered?"

Julie, however, was puzzled by something else. "A cathedral dedicated to Saint Mary Magdalene?" she asked. "Mary Magdalene wasn't a saint. She was a prostitute, a sinner. Why would a cathedral have been dedicated to her?"

And the name of the cathedral was not the only reference made in the story of Béziers to "Saint Mary Magdalene." Both my blue and my yellow books identified the date of the Béziers massacre, the first offensive of the crusade, as July 22nd, the Feast Day of Saint Mary Magdalene!

The crusaders, we learned, now hungry for more blood, had marched from Béziers toward the capital city of the Trencavels' land, Carcassonne. We followed in their path. It was late in the afternoon by the time we arrived at the Trencavel's fortified city of Carcassonne, described in our guidebook as *the most intact medieval citadel in all of Europe.* As we approached the enormous restored castle from the *autoroute,* with its blue turrets set high against the summer sky, Carcassonne looked more like an illustration from a children's fairy tale than anything real.

We entered Carcassonne's massive double stone walls at its main gate, crossing a drawbridge over a dry moat. Once inside, we were quickly overwhelmed by the huge crowd of summer tourists who had come from all over the world to see the great castle.

However, the moving sea of people, the amusement park atmosphere, and the intense heat of the afternoon sun made it almost impossible for us to appreciate the medieval architecture and exhibits. Even the colorful live jousting tournament was difficult to enjoy with the armored knights and their steeds sweating and panting in the heat.

But late in the afternoon, when the sunlight began to wane and the worn-out tourists went home dragging their souvenir swords and shields behind them, we saw Carcassonne become transformed. As if taking off its modern guise, the ancient walled city seemed to relax and revert back to the time of the Trencavels.

The costumed fire-eaters, knights and mimes dined with their families in the square, medieval musicians played softly for their own enjoyment in the castle's courtyard and dogs in the doorways of the half-timbered houses lay panting, exhausted from the day's heat.

Now, in the cool of the evening, it was easy to visualize the ancient city of Carcassonne as it had once been a vibrant city of weavers, masons, blacksmiths, artisans, *troubadours* and Cathar.

On our guided tour of the castle, we learned that the walled city of Carcassonne, the epitome of medieval military architecture, had been believed to be unassailable. Its proud history had included successful resistance of Romans, Visigoths, Moors and Charlemagne himself. But in the tremendous heat of the August sun, following the brutal fifteen-day siege of the crusaders, the city lost control of its sole water supply.

With the citizens of the city expiring in the heat and facing epidemics, the young Trencavel once again set out to negotiate with the enemy. Hoping to save the lives of his thirsty and terrified citizens, and prevent a repeat of the massacre that had taken place in Béziers, Trencavel, accompanied by nine of his faithful knights, presented himself to the crusaders. However, he was quickly taken prisoner and thrown into the deepest dungeon in his own castle, contrary to all of the period's principles of chivalry. Three months later, his city having been forcibly taken, 24-year-old Trencavel died in prison, believed to have been poisoned.

I felt inexplicably sad hearing of Raymond Robert Trencavel's fate. After we ate dinner and drank a glass of wine beneath the trees in the castle's square, we decided it was time to go, even though none of us really wanted to leave the enchanted atmosphere of the medieval city. We walked reluctantly along the perimeter of the walls in the moonlight toward where we had parked the car.

No one spoke. There was nothing to say. The massive stone, the dust beneath our feet, the stars above our heads, the cathedral spires of St. Nazaire in the distance and the shadow of the towers somehow refused to release its hold on us.

The next day, with a night of sleep, a shower, a *croissant* and a quick cup of coffee behind us, we continued on the path of the crusaders. Once again, Toby read out loud from my blue Cathar tour book as we drove. We learned that after the capture of Carcassonne, the crusaders marched on, leaving a trail of blood and wreaking havoc in their wake. They burned crops, raped, pillaged and brutally slaughtered Catholics and Cathar alike.

At one point, the crusaders took a hundred men and women as prisoners from the town of Bram, gouged out their eyes, cut off their noses, lips and ears, tied them together and sent them staggering into the next village—a warning to the Cathar and to anyone who might otherwise be tempted to protect them.

We learned that almost two full years following the fall of Carcassonne, the people of Occitania, decimated by fire and sword, were bowed but not yet broken. In the early spring of 1211, the crusaders launched a long and difficult offensive on Lavaur a town along the Tarn River, *in which the devil had taken up residence.* Our book detailed the brave story of the town, a thirteenth-century refuge for Cathar, and the tragic story of its noblewoman, Giralda de Lavaur. Captured during the attack on her town by the cruel Simon de Montfort, appointed leader of the crusade after the seize of Carcassonne, Giralda de Lavaur was brutally raped by his foot soldiers, stoned and then thrown into a well with her hands tied behind her back.

"It was a great sorrow and crime," said the *Chanson de la Croisade des Albigeois,* a medieval epic poem often quoted in my blue book, "for Dame Giralda was a good and charitable lady. Never did paupers who met her go away without alms."

When Giralda's brother, a Southern noble, learned of the threat to his sister's town, he had rushed to her rescue, accompanied by eighty knights. However, they arrived too late to save her and were captured themselves. Then, despite the chivalric standards of the period, they were hung, all eighty knights side by side in the town square.

"Never in the history of Christianity," continued the *Chanson,* "was such a high-ranking noble hung with so many knights at his side."

On the same day that Giralda, her brother, and the eighty knights met their deaths, as many as four hundred Cathar were burned at the stake at the center of Lavaur, in the largest fire of the crusade.

"I just can't understand how all this happened without any of us ever hearing about it," pondered Toby as we stood on the Place du Plô, once the site of the town's castle, where beneath our feet Giralda de Lavaur lied buried for all eternity.

As I nodded my head in agreement with Toby suddenly a violent shiver shot through my body. I turned to look for Bill but did not see him. I tried to steady myself by closing my eyes hoping to stop the swirling sensation I was experiencing.

When I opened my eyes again what I saw in front of me was the horrific sight of a man hanging from a rope on a thick wooden post. The man's throat was cut and blood was pouring from the wound. I quickly looked away, revolted, but the spectacle that surrounded him was even more horrifying. There were other bodies hanging and bleeding, and people with haunted terrified faces were running and screaming in all directions. Fires burned everywhere, and thick black smoke clouded the air.

Terrified by the scene, I turned back to the man hanging from the post in front of me now inexplicably drawn to look more closely at him. I saw the fine leather of his boots, the shiny buckle of his belt, his pale woven tunic now drenched in blood. When my gaze rested on his face, the sight no longer frightened me. Instead, I found myself struck by the beautiful pallor of his skin, the soft wave of his hair and the sweetness of his mouth. As it slowly dawned on me that this man was no stranger, a searing scream surged from the depths of my being—one I did not recognize as my own.

"Hey, hey, hey!" I heard Bill call out. As I felt his arms encircle me, my body collapsed.

'What?" asked Julie some time later as we sat in the car just outside the remains of the town wall. "What did you see?"

I didn't want to answer. I never again wanted to feel the pain I had experienced when I recognized the dead man hanging from the rope. He was the man I had seen at the castle of Puivert. The man I had watched from the window ride away forever from all that he loved.

I could not explain what kept happening to me wherever the Cathar and the nobles who had protected them had lived and died. I could not explain that this man was no stranger to me, that this land was not foreign, that this story was not unfamiliar. I only knew, deep within me, that it was so.

Each succeeding day our relationship with the medieval Cathar deepened. "I feel like I am lost in a dream or as if I've fallen into some other reality," said Julie one afternoon. "I feel like I know these people, like I've always known them and that there is some reason I'm renewing my acquaintance with them."

Toby and Bill agreed that they felt similarly. I knew that I did. And we went on, wandering among the ruins of Roquefixade, still silently keeping watch over the road from Foix to Mirepoix, exploring the perfectly preserved *Weavers* hilltop town of Cordes-sur-Ciel and drinking Fitou from paper cups at a picnic table on the banks of the Ariège River.

One day I lost my camera in the crumbling vestige of the once elegant and hauntingly beautiful Coustaussa, but later found it where I had dropped it among the iris and wildflowers.

Often after spending the day touring Cathar country, we would return to the city of Toulouse, about a ten-minute drive from our village of Cugnaux, for dinner. We enjoyed eating at a restaurant called Carpaccio's on the Place Wilson, where the food was delicious, the bread warm and the *vin de pays* wonderful. The outside tables offered us an excellent vantage point from which to watch the sophisticated Toulousians coming and going, and to enjoy the relaxing sounds to the plaza's fountain.

Prior to the crusade, red-bricked Toulouse on the river Garonne had been one of the largest medieval cities in the Western world, the capital of Occitania, and the city whose bitter defeat had represented the final and fatal blow to the South.

According to the yellow book, medieval Toulouse had been a city based on the concept of *partage*, a social system founded on the ideals of independence, honor and tolerance. It was a city of bold and diverse ideas where Christians, Jews and Muslims had lived side by side and worked together in peace. It was also a city of cultural excellence in which the art of the *troubadours* and the faith of the Cathar had flourished.

Despite long, brave efforts to defend itself, the proud city, like all the cities of the South, had eventually succumbed to the Church, and the once powerful Count of Toulouse had been forced to sign an unconditional surrender.

In 1233, to insure that Toulouse would never rise again, the Pope ordered the Inquisition established in the city. The goal of the Inquisition had been not only to persecute the heretics, but to destroy the entire society that had allowed the heretics to survive.

In the end, the Inquisition, ironically entrusted to the Dominican friars, founded by St. Dominic who had been fiercely committed to peace, proved to be the Church's ultimate weapon. The Inquisitors assigned militia to patrol the cities and countryside, appointed armed informants in even the tiniest villages, forced children to report on the religious practices of their parents, and exhumed bodies of dead Cathar and burnt them in huge public fires built in the center of town.

Hearsay and rumors were cause for arrest, and the common-law tradition of, innocent until proven guilty, was replaced with the Inquisitional law of, guilty until proven innocent, with no possibility for defense or appeal. Confessions were obtained using torture, which included the rack and the use of hot coals. The sentence was always the same—death at the stake.

"The Inquisition was started in France?" asked Toby. "Right here in Toulouse? I'd always thought the Inquisition was started in Spain."

"That was just the continuation of what was begun here," I told him. "It seems that Occitania and all that happened to the Cathar was simply just left out of our history books."

As our conversation about the Inquisition continued on, I slowly became aware of some one close behind me breathing very heavily. When I turned around to see exactly where the sound was coming from, I was unable to identify its source. The restaurant was filled to capacity but there was no one sitting close enough to us to explain what I was hearing.

I leaned over and asked my sister who was sitting next to me if she heard what I did.

"No," she replied, puzzled.

The sound itself was unnerving. But not being able to distinguish where it was coming from was even more so. I tried to distract myself, to pay attention to the conversation and finish my *profiterole*. But the raspy even rhythm of in and out, in and out, right at the back of my neck was making my skin crawl. After awhile the sound became so disturbing I asked everyone if they were ready to leave.

Once out of the restaurant and on our way back to the car the eerie sound finally subsided.

"You OK?" Bill asked as he opened the car door for me.

"I think all the talk about the Inquisition was just starting to get to me a bit," I said. "It's so frightening."

CHAPTER SEVEN

Mysteries of the Cathar

The believer was invited to fight with all possible means
against the powers of the shadow, in order that truth might triumph
and along with it, spiritual purity, the gift of self,
and the great universal brotherhood of all beings and things.

Jean Markale, *Montségur and the Mystery of the Cathars*

EVERY DAY DURING OUR TOUR of Cathar country we learned
more and more about the Cathar and the medieval crusade against Occitania. But frustratingly our traveling always seemed to raise just as many
questions as it answered.

At the top of an extremely steep, narrow road, among the ruins of
a Cathar château called Montréal-de-Sos, not far from the town of Taras-
con, we came upon a strange story that brought to mind my experience
at Montségur. According to an eyewitness, identified by our blue book as
Bérenger Lavelanet, who had been one of the last defenders of Montségur
and whose sister, Raymonde had died there in the fire, four men had rescued a Cathar treasure from Montségur the night before the fire.

Based on this eyewitness report, the men had carried the unspeci-
fied treasure along a narrow gorge of the Hers River, a pathway now
referred to in our guidebook as the *sacred way*, and hidden it *beneath the*

castle of Montréal-de-Sos amid the remains of a bell tower, in a small cave difficult to reach.

In this cave, locally referred to as an *initiatory cave*, there is a painting on the wall dated to the thirteenth century. While the painting was difficult to make out, according to a plaque next to it, numerous experts agreed, that the drawing, which consisted of a chalice, a lance, a sword and a sequence of crosses and drops of blood, were *representative of the Holy Grail.*

"Holy Grail?" asked Julie and Toby in unison.

"Isn't the Holy Grail part of the King Arthur tradition," asked Bill. "Didn't it involve Merlin, Guinevere and the Knights of the Round Table? Wasn't it all just a fairy tale? What would the Holy Grail have to do with religious heretics in Occitania?"

None of us could answer Bill's questions, but as we climbed down out of the cave, the idea occurred to me that the Cathar had possessed a real treasure, not just something of monetary value, but something very precious, something they were willing to die to protect, something very, very threatening to the Church and something I absolutely wanted to know more about.

The enigmatic cave painting and the unexplained treasure were not the only mysteries we discovered in Cathar country. In our travels, we often came across narrow little slit windows in château keeps that were identified in our guidebooks as *solar windows.* Solar windows? Other châteaux were described as having been intentionally constructed in direct line with the rising sun on either the summer or winter solstice. Why? We weren't sure what this was all about, but both Bill and I would never forget the strange violet light at the Cathar château of Peyrepertuse.

Nearly all of the Cathar's own records were destroyed by the Inquisition and very little remained to explain their faith. But as we traveled on we eventually began to put together bits and pieces of information from the little guides we had picked up along the way. We learned that light was an essential concept to the Cathar. In fact, the group conceptualized God as the *Ultimate Source of Light.* In their view each human being was a pure spark of this divine light encased within a *skin of flesh* and cast out into the cold darkness of the material world. According to the Cathar, the purpose of life was for each individual spark to discover its true nature and find his or her way back to total union with God, the *Ultimate Source of Light.*

The Ultimate Source of Light was a very different conceptualization of God than I was use to. The Judeo-Christian God was a judgmental man who lived above the sky and was completely unrelated to humanity. I loved the spark of light concept. It felt more inspiring, more poetic, definitely more forgiving and some how more expansive than the Christian concepts of heaven and hell. It reminded me of a calendar I once had. On each page of the calendar there was a picture of Albert Einstein and a quotation attributed to him at the bottom.

One month he was shown standing at Princeton University looking at a chalkboard that displayed a formula he was working on as well as his shadow. The quotation at the bottom read, "I am going to spend the rest of my life studying light." That quotation stopped me. Here was inarguably one of the greatest minds of the twentieth century committing his life to the study of light, something the rest of us just took for granted, hardly noticed. I never turned the page of that calendar again and it remained on my wall for years.

We learned that according to the Cathar, ascending back to the original Source of the Light required a person to live a good life. This consisted of such things as simplicity, absolute truth-telling, complete non-violence, no swearing of oaths, no taking of tithes, a vegetarian diet, the regular reading of the New Testament and saying of the *Our Father*, and an unwavering commitment to the search for the way Home. Among the many differences with the teachings of the Church was the Cathar idea that the return to the Light would most likely require more than a single lifetime. In other words, they believed in reincarnation.

In addition to living a good life, the Cathar believed that a return to the Light also required a specific and incontestable *enlightening experience* transmitted through an unbroken chain of Cathar initiates. The Cathar called this very secret and mysterious transcendental ceremony, the *consolamentum* and it was their only true sacrament. Once a Cathar had received the *consolamentum* he or she was no longer referred to as a Cathar believer, but a Perfect, or in French, *Parfait* or *Perfecti*. According to what we read, the *consolamentum* somehow allowed a prepared Cathar to cross over a particular *perceptual threshold* and experience a *direct perception of immortality*. The experience stimulated revelations relating to the profound mysteries of birth, death and resurrection, and left the initiate in possession of certain magical capacities and having relinquished completely any fear of death.

I remembered that all those burned at Montségur had received the *consolamentum* and according to the official record, not one of them had been bound or forced into the fire. Every one of them had accepted the consequences of their faith willingly.

We also learned that the ceremony of the *consolamentum* could only take place on certain days of the year in buildings with specific astrological and solar orientations.

While fascinating, the Cathar *consolamentum* presented many new enigmas for us.

"I'm certain I never received any magical capacities following my Holy Communion or Confirmation at Church," joked, Toby.

"But what do they mean by, "perceptual threshold"? How was it produced? And what could possibly have occurred to leave them fearless of death, certain of their immortality?" I wanted to know.

Cathar *Parfaits*, we learned, had made their living right alongside the other citizens of Occitania, often working as weavers or as healers, proficient in the use of medicinal herbs. They tirelessly traveled together in pairs dressed in dark colored, homespun hooded capes. They tended to the sick and elderly and preached to all those who would listen. They built no churches or temples but shared their message of Light in the woods, in the open fields and in the private homes and châteaux of Occitania.

The Cathar rejected all the sacraments of the Church and rejected as well the idea that the Church hierarchy could mediate between an individual and God.

They also rejected the worship of the crucifix. "Would you worship the rope that hung your father?" they asked.

According to one of my books, the Cathar might also have participated in a ritual involving a spiritual meal.

One day while visiting the medieval village of Villerouge-Termenès we came across the story of Guillaume Bélibaste, whom Inquisition records identify as the last Cathar *Parfait* to be tried and burned at the stake.

According to a legend told in the town, in the summer of the early fourteenth century, as Guillaume Bélibaste was being tied to the stake, he had called out a strange prophecy to the onlookers. "The branches of the faith," he shouted as the flames surged beneath him, "will once again grow green when seven hundred years have passed."

Following a quick calculation, Julie and I determined that Bélibaste's prophecy had been made exactly seven hundred years prior to our visit. "That's strange," we all agreed.

"It's more than strange!" exclaimed my sister. "Here we are traveling through Cathar country seven hundred years after they were wiped from the face of the earth, learning not only about the crusade against them but about their faith. What incredible timing," she mused.

Then, one bright summer morning on our way south, we passed through the tiny village of Alet-les-Bains, once popular with the Romans because of its hot mineral springs. Though not our destination for the day, we couldn't resist stopping in the village to explore the spectacular ruins of an ancient abbey visible from the road.

The Benedictine abbey, according to my yellow book, had been built sometime around 800 C.E. During the years of unrest in Occitania, it had evidently experienced many difficulties with the Catholic Church in Rome.

One particularly bizarre episode involved a representative of the Trencavels, the family under whose jurisdiction the abbey fell. The Trencavels of Carcassonne, who were sympathetic to the Cathar, had appointed an abbot who shared their views. When the appointed abbot died and a successor hostile to the Cathar was elected, a representative of the Trencavel's rode to the abbey, broke down its doors and took the new abbot prisoner. He then organized a new election, presided over by the exhumed body of the previous abbot, and saw to it that an abbot sympathetic to the Cathar was chosen. Today, under serene skies, it was difficult to imagine such an uproar having taken place.

As Julie and I wandered through the massive carved stones scattered on the ground below the immense walls of the abbey, we marveled at the beauty of the place, only guessing what it must have looked like centuries earlier. The color of the stone, a pale ochre, was particularly beautiful.

"It's so quiet," said Julie, "I feel like I should whisper." The only sound we could hear was fast-moving water as it flowed over the rocks in a stream behind the magnificent ruin. Even our footsteps were soundless on the lush green grass floor of what had once been the abbey's cloister and chapter house.

Attached to the abbey was a twelfth-century cathedral that was amazingly intact. However, we were discouraged to find its doors locked and were left only to imagine its interior. After turning away we began walking the cathedral's perimeter where we came upon a very odd feature.

"That's odd," I said, pointing to a distinct Star of David in the cathedral's huge stained glass window.

"It's the Star of David, isn't it?" asked Julie.

I nodded. "Have you ever seen a Star of David in a Catholic church before?" I asked.

"Look," said Julie excitedly. "It isn't just on that one window—it's on all of them!"

I actually knew very little about the Star of David other than it was a symbol of the Jewish people. I knew that at some point in history, the six-pointed star had been used to identify descendents of the biblical King David.

I knew for certain that Jesus had been identified in the New Testament as a direct descendant from this king, but I didn't know why it had been important enough to mention, nor had I ever given it any thought.

I also wondered what those Stars of David were doing in a Catholic cathedral in the south of France, right in the heart of Cathar country.

That night, after everyone had gone to bed, I found myself unable to sleep. After tossing and turning for what must have been more than an hour, I finally got up. Silently I made my way into the living room.

Without turning on any lights, I pulled my rocking chair up to the window where I could see out into the night. My thoughts were a jumble of questions. The strange Star of David windows at the abbey of Alet-les-Bains were just one more Cathar country mystery to add to the list of enigmas that currently included the strange Cathar sacrament of the *consolamentum*, the identity of the treasure rescued from Montségur the night before the fire, the architectural techniques involving the use of light, the involvement of the legend of the Holy Grail, and the association of Mary Magdalene to the story of Occitania and the Cathar.

If anyone three months ago had asked me about Mary Magdalene, I would have answered their questions with total confidence. I would have explained that before meeting Jesus, she had been a prostitute, a fallen woman, a shameful outcast in her society. She was a sinful woman who sold sexual favors. I had learned all I knew about Mary Magdalene from the nuns and priests who were the teachers of my childhood.

Mary Magdalene, always depicted wearing red with her long hair flowing, was the woman held up by nuns and priests as a perfect example of what would happen to all of us girls if we were not very, very careful. If we did not hide our developing adolescent bodies, repress any thoughts relative to our emerging sexuality, stay far away from the boys and confess any transgressions immediately to the priest, we, too, might become fallen.

As I sat alone in the darkness thinking about Mary Magdalene, I remembered a day I had long ago forgotten. It was without doubt one of the most embarrassing days, one of the most humiliating days of my life.

I must have been in either fifth or sixth grade at Sacred Heart School. One morning a week the priest would come to our classroom to teach religion. All the girls had been warned repeatedly by Sister Jerome not to comb their hair while the priest was in our classroom.

On this particular day, however, I had forgotten and absentmindedly pulled a large plastic yellow comb from my desk and ran it through my hair as the priest in the front of the room quizzed us with questions from *The Baltimore Catechism*. When finished, I returned the comb to my desk, never giving it a second thought.

But as soon as Father left the class, I was called by Sister Jerome to her desk. "Bring your comb," she ordered tersely. Hearing her call my name and then saying the word "comb" nearly stopped my heart. Once I was standing at her desk in the front of the room, she asked me to hand her the comb and then turn to face the class. As the rest of my classmates snickered and jeered, she proceeded to tape the comb to the top of my head and instructed me to keep it there for the rest of the day.

I wanted to die. Right there I wanted my life to be over, finished. I never wanted to take another breath again. At recess I tried to hide the comb under the hood of my winter jacket without success, and was tormented by the other children on the playground. As I thought back on this awful experience I imagined the nun was trying, in her own perverted way, to save me from becoming Mary Magdalene.

I hated her that day and would never forget her cruelty. The memory had left me filled me with a terrible shame and an unspeakable dread that no declarations of Hail Marys or Our Fathers could dispel.

Somehow as the years had gone by, I had pushed this memory and others like it away. But now, as I sat in the dark, I recognized the fear that had always been with me. It was a fear that one day I might find myself, for reasons I didn't understand, condemned to the same tragic fate of the sinner, Mary Magdalene. Did all girls educated in Catholic school face the same fear, I wondered? Did all girls despite where they were educated feel the same way?

Certainly not if they had grown up here in France. Here in France, evidently no one had ever been afraid of becoming Mary Magdalene. In fact, the "fallen woman" with the long unbound hair was actually considered a saint. She had her own feast day! Here she was honored and celebrated; sacred buildings were even dedicated in her name.

At least one great cathedral in the city of Béziers had been dedicated to her, and perhaps there were others. Here in France, obviously people thought about Mary Magdalene in a way that was quite different from the way I had been taught to think of her. How could the same fallen woman that I had been warned against be considered a great saint? It made no sense.

As I thought back on everything I had learned about Mary Magdalene since coming to France, I remembered that the crusade against the Cathar had been initiated on her feast day and that thousands of people had been murdered by the crusaders in the cathedral named in her honor. Of course, this might have been only a coincidence. But somehow I knew that it wasn't. Somehow I knew something else was going on, and I was determined to find out what it was

The next night after returning home quite late, Julie and I sat down together in the garden. For a while neither of us said a word. Then suddenly my sister sat up in her chair. "I'm wondering now," she said, "what could possibly have made us believe that a Church involved in something as awful as the Inquisition could have had any relationship at all with anything sacred? I'm fascinated by the Cathar claim that they possessed the true legacy of Jesus. What do you think it means," my sister asked?

"Can you believe," she continued, without waiting for my answer, "that I actually thought the Inquisition was set up by the good and benevolent Church to deal assertively with a small group of evil people who otherwise would have wreaked havoc on the civilized world? Was this some kind of brainwashing? Have I always accepted such superficial explanations? And if all of what happened to the Cathar and Occitania was actually just left out of our history lessons can you imagine the possibilities of what else might have been left out!"

While it was a profound relief to be able to share with someone else all that I had been thinking and feeling over this past several months, I suddenly felt responsible for turning my sister's vacation into a nightmare. I got up from my chair telling my sister that I'd return shortly.

"And it's impossible to blame it all on a bad Pope," called out my sister as I headed toward the house, "because according to what we were taught, the Popes were infallible, they couldn't make mistakes! No wonder we're so disconnected from anything sacred and holy in our lives today. Look at what we've been told is holy!"

I returned a few minutes later with a warm *baguette*, a round of pungent cheese and a bottle of hearty red wine from the Cathar region of the Corbiéres.

"It's no surprise that Catholics have a reputation for being heavy drinkers," said my sister refusing the wine, "They have a lot they need to forget."

CHAPTER EIGHT

The Bees at St. Tropez

There can be no such thing anymore of anonymous reality.
On the contrary, every single thing you are able
to perceive now exists for your sake and your sake alone.
Whatever comes to you through your senses is an intimate token
for you, a gift to wake you up, a sacred memento.

Peter Kingsley, *Reality*

LATER THAT NIGHT with all of us obviously exhausted, both physically and emotionally, I suggested a change of plans to which everyone agreed. We decided to put away all thoughts of Cathar country and head to one of the most famous beaches in the world—the French Riviera, known to the French as the Côte d'Azur.

I went out to the car early the next morning before everyone else was awake to straighten up and throw away what we had accumulated during our previous travels. Amongst the empty water bottles, napkins and paper wrappers I found the latest addition to my Cathar library, a book I had purchased in Villerouge-Termenès and then forgotten about.

I picked it up off the back seat, got out of the car and sat down with it on the stones of the driveway, already warm from the early morning sun. While I'd promised myself to put away all thoughts of the Cathar for at least the next week, until Julie and Toby went home, I couldn't resist just taking a peek at it.

The new book, like my other two Cathar tourist books, had beautiful photographs of the Cathar châteaux. There was one of Montségur in the snow and one of a spectacular sunset at Puivert.

I stopped turning the pages of the book when I came to a section with the heading, "Cathar Religion." The first sentence read, "The Cathar regarded themselves as the true heirs to the original legacy of Jesus. The orthodox Church, in their view, was a corrupt organization with purely political aims."

My attention captured, I read on.

When I came to a sentence that read, "While it is difficult to understand a religion known only through the writings of its enemies, authentic Catharist texts being extremely rare, the forbidden Cathar faith most likely evolved out of the ancient mystery schools of Egypt, Chaldea, Greece and Israel." I stopped. Evolved out of the what? That's enough, I told myself. I need a break from all this.

Back in the house, everyone was awake, dressed and excited by the prospects of the day. While our southerly direction forced us to drive through Cathar country, we all seemed to want to avoid the subject. I actually turned my head when we drove past Carcassonne, clearly visible from the *autoroute*.

After a five-plus-hour drive, we arrived at the sea. While the weather on the Côte d'Azur was quite hot, with crowds of sun worshipers, the sun, the sea and the jasmine-scented winds of Provence were a balm to our badly bruised psyches.

We found a beautiful little hotel in the cypress-covered hills above Antibes, unpacked, and settled in. Soon, the medieval ghosts that had haunted us for the past week began to take their leave. The images of hunted mystics, the pounding hooves of horses on military campaigns, and the repugnant stench of funeral pyres drifted away on the warm breezes blowing off the Mediterranean's shimmering waters.

For the next few days, we shopped for local perfumes, ceramics and paintings in the bleached stone villages. We explored the museums of Chagall and Picasso and a perfume factory in Grasse. We drank coffee on a hotel terrace which hung off the perched village of Eze, looking out at what I was certain had to be the most beautiful view of the Mediterranean in the world.

By three o'clock each day we were on the beach lolling in the aqua-colored afternoon sea, allowing the warm water to lap listlessly over us. And after feasting each night on fresh fish and vegetables smothered in olive oil and garlic *à la Provencal*, we slept dreamlessly beneath Van Gogh's starry night skies.

One afternoon, we decided to drive into the hills above St. Tropez and have a picnic. As we drove, I spotted a beautiful grove of oak trees not far from the road. "That's the place," I announced.

We parked the car and I ran ahead of the rest to select the ideal place to set up among the oaks. It was amazing to me later that I failed to notice that the grove was humming with life. As I ran, anxious to get set up before the others arrived, I was suddenly halted by a fierce burning sensation on my sandaled feet. It was only as I gasped in pain and turned to run that I realized that the ground was swarming with bees!

I stumbled back to the car, where I sat trembling as Bill tried to remove the dozens of stingers from my feet. I began to cry uncontrollably, and Bill, now alarmed, asked, "Are you in that much pain?"

To both his astonishment and mine, I tearfully responded that my tears were not the result of the bees' fiery stings, but rather because so many bees had given up their lives to protect their queen.

"It's not their fault," I sobbed. "It's not their fault! They're innocent!"

My husband looked at me quizzically. "Their fault?" he asked. I could see that he was wondering whether I was joking. Even worse, had my mind been affected by the trauma, or the bees' poison?

His questioning look made me cry even harder. "I don't know what I'm talking about! What am I saying?" I sobbed.

Finally, as everyone returned to the car, we headed off in search of a safer spot for lunch. "Just try to calm down," Bill said. "I'll find a place for us to eat. You rest."

As we drove through the hills, the burning pain in my feet began to subside. After awhile I closed my eyes and finally, lost in the rhythm of my breathing, fell into a deep sleep.

While I slept, I dreamed I was walking in a very dark forest. I couldn't see a thing in front of me and had to use my hands to feel my way through the trees. I could hear the sounds of running water alongside me—probably a stream, I thought, somewhere nearby. I was very tense, imagining anything could jump out at me from the darkness at any moment. I was also afraid that I might put my hand down on something slimy and dangerous, something that would hurt me.

All of a sudden, I could see light, and hurried toward it. In the distance I began to make out the peculiar figure of a man swathed in a beam of moonlight. He was illuminated from within by a strange iridescent light. As I came closer I could see that the man was dressed in a rich crimson gown of velvet that fastened at his neck with what looked like a golden Star of David. His long, auburn hair hung down upon his shoulders, except for small wisps of braids which were twisted up and held to his head with tiny pearls.

Atop his head, he wore a very unusual, primitive-looking jeweled crown. The jewels on the crown, while quite large, were uncut and roughly seated. At his side was a golden scepter that blossomed at the top into a three-petaled flower that looked vaguely familiar to me.

As I watched him, I began to notice that as he stood there in the moonlight, hundreds of dazzling golden bees were crawling all over him. Suddenly, he raised his arm and gently shook it. The bees, seeming to absorb his light as they would pollen, flew off, leaving a trail of pulsating light behind. For some reason, I was strangely exhilarated by the sight of those illuminated bees flying off into the dark forest.

After a moment or so, the man, who appeared to be of royal stature, lowered his arm. Then, to my shock, he looked over at me. While I felt as if I was quite far away from him, his gaze was so deep and penetrating it seemed as if there was no distance at all between us.

I awoke abruptly with a start. Bill had just stopped the car, and I slowly recalled that I was on the Riviera with my family.

"You OK?" Bill asked when he saw I was awake. "How're your feet? Think you can walk or do you want me to carry you? Are you hungry?"

"I'm all right, "I murmured, still caught in the emotions of the dream. I stared out the window at the passing scenery until we pulled into our new picnic spot. It provided a fabulous view of the sea and the afternoon turned out to be a delight.

By the end of the day, the swelling in my feet had gone down and the pain had subsided. The feelings produced by my dream, however, persisted. My memory of the king, of the tiny golden bees, of the quality of the light, of the odd crown on the king's head, refused to leave.

The next day, tan, relaxed and very well fed, we reluctantly agreed it was time to head home. Julie and Toby's return to the States, whether any of us liked it or not, was only two short days away.

The morning after our return to Toulouse, we reluctantly took my sister and her husband to the airport. Their presence had been healing and supportive, and I was sorry to see them leave,

That afternoon, while straightening up Nicholas' room, I came across a French history text book he had been reading. As I was distractedly paging through it, curious as to whether or not it would mention the Cathar, I stopped my browsing and caught my breath. I found myself looking at a portrait of an ancient French king. Embroidered in golden thread on his scarlet robe were hundreds of tiny golden bees! The picture immediately brought to mind my dream.

On the man's head sat a crown exactly like the one I had dreamed about, with identical un-faceted jewels. The golden scepter at his side was also identical! I was astounded! I knew that I had never opened this book before—in fact, I hadn't seen it prior to today.

Eagerly I read the caption. It described the king as a descendant of the original French royal dynasty, a family known as the Merovingians. At the top of his scepter, the caption explained, was the *fleur de lys*, a symbol given the first Merovingian by an angel! In almost every way this man was exactly like the man in my dream.

With all the strange events that had happened to me since moving to France, nothing had prepared me for this one! My encounter with the medieval inhabitants at Montségur, all of my subsequent experiences at the Cathar châteaux were inexplicable. But a character from a dream showing up in a history text book was just too much! How could this possibly be a coincidence?

Where might I have seen the image of the king? And what about the crown and the scepter? If I hadn't actually seen them, how could I have dreamed them?

While this bizarre coincidence frightened me a bit, I was equally fascinated. One unusual experience was following another, as if leading me down a certain path. What on earth, I wondered, was going to happen to me next?

The next day, Bill returned from work with a surprise for me. "It's a computer," he announced as he pulled the components out of the box, "your very own. A guy at work is going back to the States and he asked me if I wanted it. I'm going to set it up for you so you can do research on the Internet. Cool, huh?"

"It'll be great, Mom!" said Rachel. "You can look up everything you want about the Cathar and the Merovingians."

"And whatever else you become obsessed with," added Nicholas smartly.

That night, Bill hooked everything up and wrote down directions for me to connect to the Internet. I waited until the next day however when I was alone to try it out.

The following morning, when the house was totally quiet and there was no one around to watch me, I typed in Merovingian and in a moment I went from having no way to find anything out about the Merovingians to having more information than I would have dreamed possible.

It did not however take me long to realize that even with the power of my new computer at my fingertips, figuring out who the Merovingians were would not be easy. I found their history, not unlike that of the Cathar, to be laced with fantastic myths and wild legends and very difficult to sort out. Initially, the most I could be certain of was that a powerful tribe of Franks who called themselves the Merovingians had ruled large areas of land during the 5th through the 7th centuries in what is today France, Belgium and Germany. From this point on, distinguishing fable from fact was virtually impossible.

According to one story I came across, the first king of the Merovingian line, Mérovée, descended from a sea creature called a *quinotaur!*

Some of the French sources of information I looked at referred to the Merovingians as the, *Merovingians Magique* or Magical Merovingians, and ascribed extraordinary capabilities to them. Their incredible skills were said to include such things as clairvoyance, telepathy, the capacity to heal by the laying on of hands, and the ability to live exceptionally long lives.

All the kings were reputed to possess sacred blood and every one of them wore their hair unshorn throughout their entire lives. Interestingly, according to legend, they all shared a common birthmark, imprinted either over their shoulder or directly beneath their heart, which closely resembled an equal-sided red cross. Coincidently this equal-sided cross was not unlike the red cross displayed everywhere throughout Cathar country which had once been the coat of arms of the Counts of Toulouse, the most powerful nobles of Occitania.

As I continued my research on the Merovingians, a new question occurred to me. For no other reason than the strange way I had been introduced to both the Cathar and the Merovingian, I began to wonder if they might somehow be connected to each other. While the Merovingians had reigned centuries before the Cathar had lived in Occitania, I had a sense there was some connection, some obscure, unobvious connection. Was it possible?

One day, I came upon something in my reading that absolutely astounded me. I learned that a tomb of a Merovingian King, currently on display at the British Museum in London, had been discovered somewhere in Belgium in the seventeenth century. While there was nothing surprising about the discovery of the tomb itself, its contents fascinated me.

The tomb contained, along with many other strange items, a crystal ball and hundreds of tiny, solid gold bees. The Merovingians, it seemed, had used the bee as their royal symbol!

Was it mere coincidence that, after being stung by a swarm of angry bees at St. Tropez, I had dreamed of a Merovingian King in full regalia, having never had even heard the word, Merovingian, before? And now I was learning that these people had used the bee as their royal insignia! How was this possible?

Eventually, I came across some other very interesting information. It seemed that the Merovingians had actually been pivotal in making the Catholic Church the tremendously powerful organization it came to be.

I thought I'd left the Church behind with the Cathar, but here it was showing up again.

Apparently, the events that brought distinction to the Merovingians involved an early fifth century historic alliance made between a powerful

Merovingian King named Clovis, and someone identified as the Imperial Christian Bishop of Rome.

Yet another mystery, I thought, shaking my head. Although I'd been brought up Catholic and educated in Catholic schools. I had never heard of anyone called the Imperial Bishop of Rome.

CHAPTER NINE

The Magical Merovingians

> Like signal fires of the olden times, when lighted
> and extinguished by turns upon one hilltop after another,
> conveyed intelligence along a whole stretch of country,
> so we see a long line of initiates from the beginning
> of history to our own times communicating the word
> of wisdom to their direct successor.
>
> Manley P. Hall, *The Secret Teachings of All Ages*

WHEN BILL CAME HOME from work that night, I asked him if he had ever heard of an Imperial Bishop of Rome, but he wasn't able to offer me any help.

"Oh, by the way," he said. "I gave our phone number to a guy at work today whose wife is going to be calling you. She belongs to an organization for Americans in Toulouse and she wants to invite you to tea."

"I didn't come to France to sit around with a bunch of Americans drinking tea," I replied rather testily. But as I thought about it, the idea actually held some appeal. The next day, I received a phone call from Anne Hill, who invited me to her home the following day where the tea was to be held. "There will be women here from all over the world," she said, "the only common denominator will be that everybody will be speaking English."

For some reason, talking to Anne made the idea of tea actually sound fun and I decided to go. The Imperial Bishop of Rome, I thought, can wait another day.

The next afternoon, I was met at the door by Anne, my hostess and the current president of an organization called Americans in Toulouse. Hailing from San Diego, she had been living here with her husband for the past three years.

Her house was absolutely beautiful, decorated with lovely French antiques. I was immediately welcomed into the group and soon discovered that, while many of the women were from the States, there were also several British women and a few from Australia and New Zealand, as well as France, Italy, Germany and Holland.

The purpose of the tea, which technically should have been called a wine as almost everyone was drinking wine and not tea, was to assist these women in making new lives for themselves and their families here in France. To my surprise, I found the conversations with the English-speaking women not only comfortable, but very enjoyable. I picked up some practical tips, albeit a bit trivial in light of my recent interests, from the American women, eager to share their experiences with a newcomer.

I found out where to buy peanut butter, which I been searching for unsuccessfully, the location of a bookstore that stocked a large selection of English-language books, and the name of a laundry product that removed unwanted color from white clothing.

I also found an explanation for how I had turned one entire load of my family's white laundry pink, and another load yellow. A woman from a suburb right outside Boston explained that unlike American washing machines that take hot water directly from the hot water pipe, French washing machines heated the water inside the machine. So while you could get away with washing light colors together in the States because the water never got that hot, in France the hot water was almost boiling. That explained why most of Bill's white socks and tee shirts were currently pink.

Late in the afternoon, I became involved in a conversation about interesting local places to explore. "About forty-five minutes from here," said a woman with a delightful British accent, "is a fascinating ruin of a fortress that once provided sanctuary to medieval heretics. It's a bit of a climb up the mountain, a steep climb actually, but well worth the effort," she said.

While no one else in the group seemed particularly interested in a steep climb up a mountain to see where heretics had once lived, I could scarcely contain my excitement. As soon as I could politely do so, I picked up my glass of wine and made my way through the group to the woman who had most certainly been describing Montségur.

"Hi, I'm Chris Plant," she said, offering her hand to me as I came up beside her.

"That was Montségur you were describing, wasn't it?" I asked, taking her outstretched hand in mine, but forgetting to introduce myself.

"You know it?" asked Chris, astonished. We quickly moved through the usual questions: Who are you? What are you doing in France? How long will you be here?

I instantly felt at ease with her. Chris explained that she was in France indefinitely; her husband was employed by Rolls Royce and was making airplane engines for Airbus Industries in Toulouse.

Then, with the formalities behind us, the voices and activities in the room faded I asked the question I was most interested in. "What do you know about the Cathar?"

I had never dreamed of running into someone at a tea who knew anything about the Cathar. Chris, to my amazement, not only knew about them, but seemed to have an interest very much like my own.

She then said something that startled me. A short time ago, she reported, she had developed an "irrational preoccupation" with the Cathar. "It began directly following a car accident," she explained, "which really shook me up, not physically, but emotionally. I wasn't hurt but I really haven't felt the same since. The following day while resting, I picked up a book that a colleague of my husband had given to him. It was a book about the Cathar. I learned that the fire at Montségur had taken place on the same day as my accident, March 16th. Since then, I've hardly been able to concentrate on anything else. My husband thinks I've gone completely mad, and sometimes I think he's right. I spend almost every afternoon reading anything I can find about these people. And I've no explanation whatsoever for why I suddenly developed this interest."

We then proceeded to fall into a deep conversation, forgetting about the other guests and failing to notice when the afternoon sun started to set and the other guests began departing. We spoke about Puivert, Arques and Peyrepertuse. We spoke about the horror of the crusade and its many mysteries. By the time we realized the late hour, Anne was straightening up and all the other guests had gone home.

"Well," laughed Anne as Chris and I came to offer her our thanks, "it certainly seems that you two have found a common interest. What have you been talking about all afternoon?"

"The Cathar," Chris replied.

"The what?" asked Anne. "Oh, you mean the heretics? I've seen their names on the road signs, but I don't know a thing about them. Do you?" she inquired of both of us.

"A bit," I said. "But what is really important is that now I know I'm not the only person in the world fascinated by French heretics. And I have you to thank for that, Anne. Thank you so much for calling and inviting me to your home for this tea."

As Chris and I said good bye to Anne and walked out to our cars, she turned to me and asked, "You meant Occitan heretics, didn't you? They weren't French."

"Yes, right, they were Occitan," I replied.

"Did you know that the Cathar believed in reincarnation?" asked Chris.

I nodded.

"Have you ever considered that in a past life you might have been a Cathar yourself and that maybe it's the reason you have become so pre-occupied with the group?" Then, as if she didn't expect an answer from me, she continued, "Let's speak on the phone again tomorrow, shall we? I'll ring you as soon as I get home from my watercolor class."

On the drive home, I considered Chris' question. I'd read that the Cathar believed in reincarnation, but I wasn't sure whether or not I believed in it. How could anyone know for certain? What I was sure of was that I could barely wait to speak to her again. I wondered what books she had read and if she had any explanation for any of my recent experiences. I also wondered if she knew anything about the Merovingians. I had so many questions I wanted to ask her.

When we spoke on the phone the next day, I told Chris about my strange experiences at Montségur and Puivert, and about my dreams that included the young girl.

"Oh, my gosh!" Chris replied. "That's amazing! Who do you think she is?"

Then I told her about my more recent encounter with the Merovingians, and asked if she knew anything about them.

"I'd never even heard of the group prior to getting stung by the bees at St. Tropez," I said. "Then I find out that the king in my son's history book is wearing the same crown and carrying the same scepter as the one in my dream—and that he's from the first royal dynasty of France, who just happened to use the symbol of the bee as their royal insignia."

"You know," Chris replied, "now that I'm thinking about it, I remember seeing a tomb of a Merovingian king once in the British Museum. The tomb, as I remember it, had been found in Belgium and contained a lot of strange things, including hundreds of tiny bees made of solid gold."

"Yes, I've read about that tomb as well. What I'm most interested in at the moment is the Merovingians' connection with the Catholic Church. Do you know anything about it?" I asked eagerly.

"The Merovingians had a relationship with the Church? What kind of relationship?" she asked, bewildered.

"That's what I'm trying to understand," I replied. "Something I read said that the group had been instrumental in the Church's rise to power.

"Well, I'm afraid I'm useless in that regard. But I do have a friend here in Toulouse, another Brit," said Chris, "who knows a lot about French history. Perhaps Alicia could help you make some sense of the Merovingians and their bees. I could invite both of you to my house and you could speak with her. Would tomorrow night work for you?"

"I'll be there," I told her with certainty. Nothing could have kept me away.

The next evening, I arrived a bit early at Chris' home, eager to meet her friend, Alicia. "I thought we'd sit outside, it's such a beautiful evening," said Chris as she led me through her living room towards a wide open glass door and then to a chair at a table in her garden.

She then returned to the house, calling back, "Alicia should be here any minute. You'll be amazed by how much she knows. I'll just get us some tea."

As I waited for her return and for Alicia's arrival, my attention was drawn to the brilliant colors and fragrant perfumes of Chris' well tended garden. Deep blue periwinkles, jewel-colored anemone, and crimson dahlias glowed in the fading light. Beyond the garden were fields of colorless wild grasses parched by the summer sun, and in the distance was an old barn constructed of field stone. Hawks circled overhead and for a moment I was sure that Chris' home was the most beautiful place I'd ever been.

I was so engaged enjoying the scenery that Chris' return to the garden startled me. "OK," said Chris, "here we are." She carried a teapot in one hand and a plate of cookies in the other. Close behind her followed Alicia, carrying a tray laden with pretty porcelain cups and saucers, spoons and a large round jar of honey.

After quick introductions, Alicia and Chris settled themselves around the table. Alicia's pretty face was framed by a closely cropped cap of henna-colored hair, a pair of large, blue-rimmed glasses resting on her nose. Years in Holland, New Zealand, and Majorca had given her British accent a charming cadence.

Her husband, she explained, worked in Toulouse for Cathay Pacific Airlines. "And we're in Toulouse until... well, really there's no telling how long we'll be here. It's the same for all of us Brits and Americans in Toulouse, isn't it?"

I nodded politely, not really familiar with the expatriate scene.

"I hear you've been having some pretty interesting experiences lately," she said. "Chris says you've been visiting Cathar châteaux and having strange dreams of bees and Merovingians?"

I smiled. "Yes, my life's been pretty unusual lately. I've been haunted by the heretic Cathar for months. I take it Chris told you about my encounters at Montségur and Puivert?

"Oh, dear," Chris interjected. "I hope you don't mind that I told Alicia about what's happened."

"No, no, it's fine," I said to Chris. "Anyway," I continued, turning back to Alicia, "after a dream I had in St. Tropez I've suddenly become fascinated by an ancient Frankish dynasty. Before moving to France, I wasn't even interested in history. Now I'm interested in little else!"

"You're speaking about the Merovingians, aren't you? asked Alicia. Their history isn't exactly what I'd call straightforward," she said. "I imagine you're having a rough time of it."

"At the moment," I replied, "I'm particularly interested in their relationship with the Church. I went to Catholic school but I've never heard a word about any Merovingians. Chris said you might be able to help."

"Right," said Alicia, taking a deep breath. "Well, their involvement with the Church is a pretty complex subject. I'm not sure what you already know or where I should begin…"

CHAPTER TEN

The Imperial Bishop of Rome

It is the winners who write history—their way.

Elaine Pagels, *The Gnostic Gospels*

"STORIES ALWAYS WORK BEST when started from the beginning," Chris said smiling.

"All right," Alicia agreed with a chuckle. "Well, a long, long time ago, in a place far, far away, late in the fifth century, the brilliance of the great Roman Empire was losing its glow. At that time there lived a powerful tribe of Franks who called themselves the Merovingians. Initially, they were just one of many Germanic tribes pouring in across the weakening boundaries of the Roman Empire. These tribes were collectively referred to as *barbarians* by the record-keepers, who succeeded the Imperial scribes..." Alicia stopped at this point to sip her tea.

"Imperial scribes?" Chris asked. "You mean the Romans?"

"Right," replied Alicia.

"And who succeeded the Imperial scribes?" I asked.

"The Catholic Church," said Alicia. "After the Romans, the Catholic Church became the primary record keepers of Western Civilization. At the same time that the Roman Empire was being overtaken on all its frontiers and no longer had the resources or will to defend itself, Christianity had been developing into a well-structured political system. In fact, its internal order had been designed to closely resemble the Roman hierarchy of power. After nearly four centuries of leadership by Paul in Jerusalem, Jerome in Constantinople, Augustine in Africa, and Leo the Great in Rome, supported by pro-Christian imperial policy, the Church was positioned perfectly to slip into the vacuum created by the collapsing Roman Empire."

I was extremely impressed by the scope of Alicia's knowledge, but I was also having trouble following her theme. Considering the Church as a political structure was virgin territory for me.

"When the city of Rome itself was on the brink of falling and its citizens were fleeing to the countryside," she continued, "the Church seized the opportunity to take control, and the Imperial Christian Bishop of Rome stepped up to claim it. He never would have been successful, however, without support from the Merovingian military."

"Wait a minute! Wait a minute!" I interrupted. "Who's the Imperial Bishop of Rome?"

"The head of the Church in Rome, of course," Alicia replied, looking a bit impatient.

"Do you mean the Pope?" I asked.

"Oh, I see your confusion," Alicia conceded. "In the early fifth century, there was no Pope as we know him today. Church leadership was shared by bishops scattered throughout the major cities of Western Europe and Byzantium. I think the Bishop of Rome might have started calling himself Pope or *Papa* late in the fourth century, but the title initially wasn't to imply that it was the supreme head of the Church."

"You're mistaken on this point, Alicia," I interrupted again, "the apostle, Peter, was the first Pope of the Church. Jesus himself handed leadership directly over to him before the crucifixion! I am certain of that."

"Right. You may have learned that in religion class. I guess we all did. But it actually wasn't that simple," replied Alicia, the tone of her voice softening. "The truth is, the position of Pope as the head of the Church evolved over a long period of time. Anyway, what's important here," she continued, is that with the city of Rome about to fall, military support was all the Church needed to ensure its political fortune. So the Imperial Bishop of Rome turned for help to the French Merovingians, who were renowned as highly skilled warriors and military strategists.

"A partnership between the Church and the Merovingians was actually quite logical," she continued, warming to her subject. "The Merovingian King, Clovis, who lived in what is today Northern France, had a devout Christian wife who was on very friendly terms with a powerful French Christian bishop. More important, however, was the fact that while neither King Clovis nor the rest of the Merovingians were Christians, their claim to possess the true mystical legacy of Jesus was widely recognized as greater than or at least equal to the Church's own."

"What do you mean by that?" asked Chris.

"I can't explain it but there are many references to this fact in the historical record," replied Alicia. "I do know that the Merovingian kings never involved themselves with the actual administration of their kingdoms and that they were called priest-kings, in the tradition of the priest kings of ancient Egypt.

"I also know that the name of the bishop who negotiated the agreement between King Clovis of the Merovingians and the Imperial bishop of Rome was Rémy. He was later canonized a saint for his efforts. In exchange for military protection, the Imperial Bishop of Rome agreed to share the legacy of Jesus with the Merovingians. He promised Clovis that the Merovingians would be recognized as the secular heads of the Christian Church for all time. In fact, it was actually this agreement that made the Church the powerful organization it came to be.

To seal their agreement, Clovis consented to be baptized. The famous baptism took place in the French town of Reims before thousands of witnesses on a cold Christmas morning in the year 496."

"I remember hearing the story of Clovis' baptism in history class," put in Chris. "But I'm sure I never heard anything about the Church agreeing to share the legacy of Jesus with the Merovingians."

"Right," agreed Alicia. "That's because, while it's widely known that Clovis and his warriors gave military support to the Church, very few people really understand the agreement made between the two groups. The church later downplayed the fact that the Merovingians were to share the legacy of Jesus. The truth is, as the Church became more and more powerful on its own, the Merovingians and their agreements with the Church simply slipped into complete oblivion."

At this point I stopped listening. The story Alicia was telling was complete nonsense! I'd never heard of Clovis. I'd never heard of St. Rémy. And the part about Peter not being the first Pope was completely wrong.

Alicia was trashing major Church doctrine. This was not just a military crusade in the medieval south of France that had been omitted from Church history. Apostolic succession was a fundamental part of Church doctrine—the very reason Popes were believed throughout history to be infallible. It was in the Apostle's Creed, recited out loud at Mass by all Catholics every Sunday, an essential element of their belief.

"Hold on!" I finally interrupted. "Can we go back to this Imperial Bishop of Rome business again? I'm still having trouble with it. Isn't there a quote from Jesus in the New Testament that establishes Peter as the first Pope? It says, "Thou art Peter and upon thy rock I will build my Church.""

"Oh, that," replied Alicia. "That was just a later addition in the New Testament, brought in to justify Rome's authority. The Roman Emperor, Constantine, was actually the person who established the office of the Imperial Bishop. He appointed an Imperial Bishop in Rome, one in Alexandria, and one in Constantinople. Before that, there were bishops scattered all over the Christian kingdom with equal status, but there was no established central leadership. Constantine made his appointments soon after his infamous political decision to endorse Christianity in the middle of the fourth century. Directly following he called together the Council of Nicea, for the purpose of defining and consolidating Christian doctrine."

"Oh, come on! Now are you going to say that Constantine's conversion to Christianity was purely a political maneuver?" I asked unbelievingly. "Didn't he convert to Christianity after having a miraculous vision of Christ on a battlefield? Didn't he then inscribe a dedication to Christianity on his shield—*Invictus*... something or other?"

"Right," said Alicia. "*In hoc signo vinces*. In Latin it means, *Under this sign, I will conquer*. However, the symbol he actually painted on his shield was most probably related to Mithra, not to Jesus."

"Who was Mithra?" asked Chris curiously.

"He was a very popular pre-Christian god of the Roman Empire—one who, ironically, had the same birthday as Jesus. It's my understanding," said Alicia, "that Constantine was interested in Christianity purely as a vehicle to forge internal unity amongst all the peoples of the vast Roman Empire."

Despite my frown, Alicia continued. "His public endorsement of the religion enabled him to establish himself as the supreme sovereign over both secular and religious life. He was actually instrumental in constructing the Christianity that we know today."

"I'm not sure I want to hear any more of this," I said nervously, certain that even more of my beliefs were about to be challenged.

"It's historical fact," Alicia said calmly. "Christianity in the fourth century was very different from the homogeneous group that we think of today. While all of the groups calling themselves Christians claimed to possess the true teachings of Jesus, there were actually major disagreements amongst them.

"Perhaps the greatest involved the question of Jesus' divinity. At Nicea, Constantine made sure that this and all other arguments were resolved. After Nicea, there was only one male god represented by the trinity of Father, Son and Holy Spirit. There was one New Testament, one interpretation, and one divine Jesus, who bore little if any resemblance to a man by that name who had once lived on the shores of the Sea of Galilee. Anybody who disagreed was banished. It was as simple as that."

I listened speechlessly, my irritation increasing as Alicia continued with her story. Chris said nothing, rapt in thought.

"Following the council, Constantine had all the Bibles rewritten to highlight the new doctrine. In fact, from what I understand, there's not a single Bible in existence today that preceded this rewriting. And I've read that long after Constantine allied himself with Christianity and its representative values, he had his wife boiled in oil and his son murdered.

"Constantine wasn't even baptized until moments before his own death, which was years after his infamous conversion, and some historians question whether he was ever baptized at all."

At this point, Chris cleared her throat and pushed back her chair from the table. "I think this would be a good time to take a break, don't you? Let's have some tea, then." Without waiting for a response, she hurried off, probably seeking relief from the tense atmosphere.

Alicia and I sat together silently gazing up at the night sky. It had long ago darkened and was now sprinkled with glimmering stars. I wanted to tell Alicia that her version of history was absolutely absurd. I wanted to tell her that her story made a complete mockery of everything I'd ever been taught, everything I'd ever believed to be true. But I didn't say a word.

Thankfully Chris returned before the silence between us became too uncomfortable. "OK," she said after pouring each of us a fresh cup of tea and then settling herself back into her chair. "Are we ready to return to the Merovingians?"

"Unfortunately," said Alicia, "there isn't much more to tell. When the Church no longer needed them, the dynasty was simply disposed of."

"Disposed of? What exactly does that mean?" I asked.

"It means that initially they were reduced to insignificance, then, completely usurped. You can find references to Merovingian queens being retired to monasteries and Merovingian kings being imprisoned. At one point, the historical record simply begins referring to the once-powerful tribe of Merovingians as, *les rois fainéants*, or the *lazy kings*.

Ultimately, the entire royal bloodline was wiped out to prevent any future challenges to the Church's power. And before the dust had time to settle on the Merovingians, everything was neatly covered up. Now, as we can obviously see, they are barely remembered by anyone at all."

I sat silent, rooted in my chair as this strange panorama of history was laid out before me.

"With the Merovingians out of the way," Alicia went on, "the Church put Charlemagne's family on the French throne, a family that posed no serious threat to the Church's supremacy and carried on as if nothing had happened. Initially the Carolingians all married Merovingian queens so that…"

"Sorry to interrupt," I said, no longer able to remain quiet. "But you don't really believe that the Church actually wiped out an entire royal dynasty, do you? I don't mean to sound rude, but I don't think what you are describing is possible. Not to mention the fact that if it were true, others besides you would have heard about it."

"It is rather hard to believe," Chris put in sympathetically, "but look what the Church did to the Cathar!"

Alicia continued, oblivious to my tone. "Actually, it is very possible that the Church didn't succeed in wiping out the entire bloodline. There's a story that an infant son of a true Merovingian King named Dagobert was secretly rescued from an attempt on his life by the Church. According to this legend, the child of royal Merovingian blood is supposed to have grown up and lived out his life at a place not far from here, a place called Rennes le Château."

"So, do you think…" Chris began.

"You know," I said suddenly feeling completely overwhelmed. "I think I've had enough for one night." I pushed my chair back and stood up from the table. "Sorry," I said. "I don't mean to be rude. It's just that I've always trusted… it's just that this is all news to me."

I was at the front door when Chris caught up with me. "Are you all right?" she asked, concerned.

"I'm OK," I said, sensing that Chris was feeling a bit responsible for my being upset. "Don't worry about it. I just need some time to sort this all out. However, if any of it turns out to be true… well… then… ask me again how I feel."

I called back a goodnight to Alicia, and walked out the door. Once outside, I noticed that the night had become cloudy and the sky surprisingly dark. As I backed out of the driveway and made my way down the shadowy road, images of magical long-haired warrior kings and black robed bishops convened in the ancient city of Nicea raced through my mind.

It couldn't all be true, it just couldn't be, I assured myself as I wound around the tiny road from Chris' house to mine. Alicia must be wrong. She had to be.

That night, as I climbed into bed, I pressed myself close to Bill's dependable warmth. "Hi," he said sleepily, "It's late. I tried to wait for you but I fell asleep. Is everything OK?"

"Not really," I replied.

"Tell me about it in the morning after you've had a good night's sleep," said Bill, pulling me closer.

I snuggled beside him, closed my eyes, and slept fitfully all night long.

During the next week, I tirelessly searched the historical records for evidence to refute Alicia's contentious claims regarding the history of the early Church. My new computer was indispensable, providing me with unlimited access to both ancient and contemporary sources of information.

Despite what I had been taught about the foundations of the Catholic Church, by week's end I was forced to conclude that it was my own version of history, not Alicia's, that was incorrect. Based on my research, I had no other choice but to accept that I had been sorely misled about the first Popes, about the motives behind Constantine's conversion to Christianity, and about exactly who had defined the official doctrine of the Catholic Church and for what purposes.

From what I read, it was clear that a central Church authority had not been established until possibly as late as the fifth century of the Christian era. Jesus, in fact, had not appointed his apostle Peter as the first Pope. Further, in contrast to what I'd been taught, not even contemporary Church scholars disputed that Constantine's devotion to Christianity had been due to political ambition, rather than to his spiritual inclinations.

There was equal agreement in historical records that Constantine had personally called together the fourth century Council of Nicea solely to shape a new, improved, united Christianity with which to impose religious conformity upon his sprawling Roman Empire.

The fourth century Roman Emperor Constantine, though not a Christian himself, had called together the Council of Nicea to end the diversity in the Empire among all the different groups calling themselves Christians. Under his direction, the bishops in attendance at the council of Nicea had designed an Orthodox Christian creed with which to unify the vast Roman Empire under a single god.

And at its conclusion, these individuals had defined the supreme Christian god as a divine male trinity, completely separate from humanity and accessible only through the intercession of an all-male Church hierarchy, who saw themselves as the guardians of the *one true faith*. The divine son of God, Jesus Christ, was recognized as having been crucified, buried, and then resurrected to life on the third day for the purpose of saving humanity.

Directly following the council of Nicea, all other spiritual traditions, philosophies and literature of the ancient world as well as worship of every form of the female face of god had been outlawed. Books were burned, temples destroyed, sacred springs renamed and ancient sacred holidays like December 25th rededicated. The ancient doctrine of reincarnation was banned; the bishops of Nicea agreeing it would minimize the role of Jesus

Christ as the only savior, downplay the need for salvation in this lifetime, and diminish the unique nature of Christ's resurrection.

Late in the fourth century, any independent pursuit of spirituality was, by Imperial decree, made a crime punishable by death. The consequence of refusing to fear, respect, and obey the priests and bishops of the Church as representatives of god on earth would further result in eternal damnation.

The more I learned, the more betrayed I felt. I had grown up trusting what I'd been taught—that the fundamental beliefs of Christianity had been established by Jesus himself and passed on by an uninterrupted lineage of his own disciples. It had never entered my mind that the doctrine of the early Church had been designed—or even influenced—by a Roman Emperor intending to control individual spirituality for his own political purposes.

To make matters even worse, in my investigations of Church history I came across some of the writings of the now-esteemed St. Augustine, bishop of Hippo, who had played a principal role in further shaping the theology of the Catholic Church. It was Augustine, in fact, who created the essential Church doctrine of *original sin*.

What I read about this man astounded me. Soon after the Council of Nicea, in the early 5th century, Augustine proclaimed that mankind's deeply rooted moral weakness must be controlled. He unequivocally believed that people were basically evil and must be *compelled* to enter the Church.

This man had also been a misogynist of the highest order. Along with his friend, St. Jerome, Augustine had prohibited women from holding any leadership positions within the Church. Men alone, he determined, would constitute the body of the Christian community. After abandoning his mistress and illegitimate young son, St. Augustine wrote that only man (but not woman) was made in the image and likeness of God.

In even greater contrast to the pre-Christian view that sex was an integral part of the sacredness of life, Augustine believed that sex was intrinsically evil. He held women directly responsible for luring otherwise pious men into sinful sexual activity, and even went so far as to describe women as *vessels of excrement!*

Why had I never questioned the subservient role of women in the Church? Why hadn't I asked myself, while observing the nuns straightening the altar before Mass, why they weren't even permitted to participate in the celebration of the central ceremony of Christian life, the Mass?

Now, I felt outright stupid and ashamed of myself for having questioned so little. I had, like so many others, blindly accepted what I had been told.

My research substantiated most of Alicia's assertions about the early Church, but I was less successful learning more about the Church's dealings with the ancient tribe of Franks, the Merovingians. It was indisputable that the Imperial Bishop of Rome had, in fact, made a pact with King Clovis establishing the Merovingians as secular heads of the Church. In exchange, Clovis swore to offer military protection. It was this agreement that set the precedent for the later establishment of the Holy Roman Emperor, the temporal arm of the Papacy which prevailed until the nineteenth century.

It also seemed clear that the Church had truly played a significant role in usurping the French royal dynasty and the subsequent establishment of the Carolingians (the family of Charlemagne). The historical record was ambiguous, however, as to what exactly had become of the royal Merovingians. Had the Church actually wiped them out, as Alicia had reported?

Nor could I confirm or refute Alicia's claims regarding the Merovingian's purported entitlement to the legacy of Jesus. While I did find numerous curious references to the king's mystical proclivities, none of them specifically were linked to Jesus.

I did, however, come across a very interesting photograph of a statue of St. Rémy, the French bishop responsible for negotiating the agreement between the Church and King Clovis. What interested me about the photograph was Rémy's breastplate. The caption beneath the photograph described it as a gift given to Rémy from Clovis.

I was absolutely certain I recognized this distinctive twelve-jeweled breastplate from an illustrated Old Testament that I'd had since childhood. This garment, as I recalled, had been worn by the Hebrew priests appointed by Moses to care for the Ark of the Covenant. What, I wondered, was Clovis doing with this breastplate?

According to the canonical gospels of the New Testament, the ancestry of Jesus had derived from a lineage of Hebrew Kings which included David.

Could this breastplate be evidence of a link between the Merovingians and the legacy of Jesus?

The Cathar had also claimed to possess the true legacy of Jesus. Could there be a connection between the two groups other than they had both lived in France? I began to feel like I was trying to assemble a large complex jigsaw puzzle.

Could this piece fit here, or here? Could the Star of David, a symbol of ancient Hebrew ancestry, in the windows of the cathedral at Alet-les-Bains in the heart of Cathar country have anything to do with all of this?

One thing I knew for certain—in light of what I now recognized as the Church's ability to distort the truth, there was absolutely nothing I could be sure of regarding Christianity itself or the actual legacy of Jesus.

When I finally fell asleep that night, I once again dreamed of the girl from Montségur. She hadn't come to me in dreams for several days. As usual, she was running ahead of me, waving to me with her hands, pulling me forward with her penetrating eyes, calling to me to catch up with her.

CHAPTER ELEVEN

Secrets at Rennes le Château

Orthodox Christianity appealed to the government,
not as a religion that would encourage enlightenment
or spirituality, but rather as one that would bring order
and conformity to a faltering Empire.

Helen Ellerbe, *The Dark Side of Christian History*

THE MORNING FOLLOWING MY DREAM of the girl from Montségur, I was surprised to receive a call from Alicia, whom I hadn't spoken to since the night we had met in Chris' garden.

"Alicia, I'm so glad to hear from you," I said when I heard her voice. "I was planning on calling you."

"Really?" said Alicia. "Why?"

"I wanted to apologize to you for being so rude the other night at Chris'. I'm really sorry. I thought I knew what I was talking about but I was wrong."

"Oh, don't give it another thought," said Alicia kindly. "In fact, I was wondering if you'd like to accompany me to the village of Rennes le Château, where the surviving Merovingian heir is believed to have lived out his life. It's not far from here."

"And," she added, "the village has a very interesting history, which includes, among other things, the Cathar. There's actually some speculation that the Cathar treasure, whatever it might have been, wound up in this village after it was carried out of Montségur the night before the fire."

There wasn't a moment's hesitation on my part. "I'd love to go," I said eagerly.

"Good," said Alicia. "I'll be round to pick you up about half nine this morning."

And within an hour, we were heading south away from Toulouse on the *autoroute*. "Chris is on holiday in England. She'll wish we had postponed our trip until she was back," said Alicia, as we turned off the highway onto a narrow tree-lined road. "But I simply had to get out into the country today."

The day was bright and clear, and the brilliant morning sunlight bathed all in its path in a golden light. The tiny villages we passed along the road buzzed in morning activity. There were gray-haired old men wearing woolen berets playing *pétanque* in the village squares. Women with hair tied back in neat chignons, were shopping for the day's fruits and vegetables at the local *marché*. Others were bicycling home with their *pain de campagne* and other purchases tucked securely under their arms.

The winding road carried us deep into the foothills of the Pyrénées and then into a lush green valley. Soon we found ourselves in the familiar quiet of Cathar country, surrounded only by an endless expanse of ripening vineyards and fields of giant sun flowers, their childlike faces bent upward to bask in the morning sunshine. It never failed to amaze me how much I loved this land, how much I loved this timeless quiet.

"Alicia," I asked, "Do you know anything about a church in this area that has Stars of David in its stained glass windows?"

"You mean the cathedral at Alet-les-Bains?" she asked.

"Yes," I replied, pleased that she knew. "Any idea why a Catholic Church would have Stars of David painted on their windows?" "Not a clue," she replied. "Peculiar, huh? This whole area is riddled with mystery, isn't it? Wait until you see Rennes le Château!"

Then, keeping her eyes on the road as we drove deeper into Cathar country, Alicia filled me in on what she knew about our destination. According to her, the village of Rennes le Château, because of its natural fortifications high above the surrounding lowlands and its rare hilltop lake, had been a coveted location throughout all of ancient times.

At different periods of antiquity, the village had been home to the Celts, the Visigoths, the royal house of Aragon and was at one time under the banner of the Trencavel, of Carcassonne. Eventually, after having endured wars, the Cathar Crusade and the plague, the village had fallen into decay.

Then, in the late nineteenth century, an interesting development occurred: a young village priest named Bérenger Saunière began an extraordinary restoration project. It was extraordinary, explained Alicia, because of the elaborateness of the construction, the strange style in which he redecorated the tiny village church, and most of all, because of the mysterious manner in which the entire project had been financed.

According to Alicia, Saunière, a penniless Catholic priest living on only a tiny stipend, had built a domain fit for a nobleman and accomplished it without any apparent financial means. "No one to this day," remarked Alicia, "has been able to figure out how it was all paid for or exactly why the project was even undertaken."

One of many theories proposed to explain this mystery was that the village priest had found an ancient treasure hidden on the property that had once belonged to the Merovingians or to the Cathar. Another theory was that the priest had discovered a secret of extraordinary historical significance that wealthy individuals had paid him to keep concealed.

"Wait till you see this place!" Alicia said. "I personally think Saunière knew something important that involved the Merovingians, the Cathar and an extremely interesting medieval military order of knights. He knew a secret that for some reason he couldn't reveal, but he nevertheless felt compelled to express."

We had just reached the summit of a long and winding road, and before I could ask any questions, she pointed ahead. "Here we are."

Here we are, where? I wondered, as we made our way through a narrow opening of old stone buildings. We entered a village that looked as if it had fallen asleep long, long ago and hadn't reawakened—like many other places in Cathar country.

But the village of Rennes le Château particularly brought to mind the fairy tale of *Sleeping Beauty*, where the princess pricks her finger on a spinning wheel and the entire court falls into an enchanted sleep. While no forbidding thorns surrounded the village, the entire domain seemed under some sort of magic spell, warning visitors to proceed cautiously and at their own risk.

There was absolutely nothing welcoming in Rennes le Château. We drove past a deserted cafe called La Pomme Bleue, and a book shop with a sign overhead which read, 666.

"It's the number of the devil in Revelation," Alicia said in response to my inquiring look.

"Oh, that clears it right up," I laughed sarcastically.

Alicia brought the car to a halt at the edge of a cliff. "We'll park here," she announced.

"We're getting out?" I asked half jokingly. "Is it safe?"

An enormous panorama lay directly in front of us. In the distance was a richly diverse landscape of magnificent white mountains and green valleys, tiled red roofed villages and an endless expanse of gentle, stony plains.

To my right perched on the absolute edge of the cliff sat a very beautiful little gothic building with a crenellated tower. This one building immediately clarified why Alicia had used the word extraordinary to describe the priest's construction project.

The delicate white stone building seemed to practically hang from the precipice of the cliff. It held an aura of mystery about it, appearing as if it had been superimposed on the landscape, as if it belonged to another time or another place. Why had it been built in that precarious location, I wondered?

"It's lovely, isn't it?" asked Alicia interrupting my thoughts. "It's a Golden Building, designed in the magical proportions of the Golden Mean. Sacred geometry dictated its exact placement."

The white tower was more than beautiful. I felt attracted to it as if by a magnetic force and barely heard what Alicia had said. The golden what?

"Come on, it's only the beginning. Wait until you see the church!" said Alicia. As we turned and began our walk toward the church, Alicia told me that Saunière had called the unusual tower hanging off the cliff, *Tour Magdala.*

After Mary Magdalene? I wondered.

On the way to the church, we passed an elegant Renaissance-style house, lovely gardens and a fountain. "It must have once been very beautiful here," I observed.

Alicia nodded. "The house is where Father Saunière lived with his housekeeper, Marie, who was named the sole heir of his fortune after he died. He called the house, *Villa Bethania*. Bethany, by the way, was the name of the home of Lazarus, Mary Magdalene's brother."

This was the second structure on the property associated with Mary Magdalene. "Do you mean the Lazarus Jesus raised from the dead in the New Testament story?" I asked.

"Right," replied Alicia.

Tucking this information away, I observed a small church before us. It looked similar to many buildings of its age I'd previously seen in France. As we came closer, however, it began to reveal its very distinct character. There was an inscription written in the apex of a triangle over the entrance, and we stopped to read it.

Terribilis est locus iste.

"It's Latin," Alicia responded to my questioning look. "It means something like, *This is a terrible place.*"

"Why?" I asked, as Alicia signaled me to follow her. "Why would a church be a terrible place?"

"The church is believed to have been originally constructed and dedicated to Mary Magdalene in the seventh or eighth century," said Alicia, not answering my question.

Once inside the door, out of the bright sunlight and into the darkness of the church, we were immediately welcomed by an almost life-size statue of a hideous, hunchbacked, horned devil. The devil's vampire-like wings, sharply protruding talons, bulging, angry eyes and open mouth looked about to attack. I stifled the urge to turn around and go right back out through the door.

It was frightening, but at the same time fascinating. Looking closer, I saw that the devil held a holy water font on its back. Above it were four angels, each making one part of the sign of the cross. One kneeling angel pointed to an inscription that read, *Par ce signe tu le vaincras.*

I struggled to translate the French and then gasped. I turned to Alicia,

By this sign you will conquer him? Isn't it from the story of Constantine's conversion to Christianity?" I asked.

It struck me as more than a bit odd that I was seeing this quote after having just researched the fourth century Roman Emperor Constantine and his relationship with Christianity. "Why is it here?" I whispered to Alicia. "What does it mean? And what's the significance of the horrible-looking devil?"

Alicia simply shrugged her shoulders. "I warned you," she said. "Rennes le Château is a very strange place."

As I took a step back from the grotesque statue, my startled gaze fell upon two yellow sculptured salamanders; their fat tails curled above them, sitting atop the devil's head just beneath the angels. They reminded me immediately of the two strange salamanders I had encountered at Montségur.

All at once my head started spinning and I felt nauseated. First it was the quote from Constantine and now there were these two salamanders. It was just too much for me to absorb.

It was unquestionably the two sculpted salamanders that put me on overload. When I'd previously seen the two strangely behaving salamanders on my way down the mountain of Montségur, I'd felt certain they held some mysterious significance to me. Now, seeing the salamanders here at Rennes le Château atop the devil's head, on this hideous holy water font, in this mysterious church deep in the heart of Cathar country, I was not only reminded of the peculiar feeling I'd had before, but felt again as I had each time I'd awoken from a dream of the girl from Montségur. As odd as it seemed, I felt as if these salamanders somehow represented the signature of whatever strange force was calling me to follow.

When I eventually regained my composure, I turned away from the salamanders to face the front of the church. I was immediately bombarded by a cacophony of wild colors, flamboyant decorations and confusing surreal images, all of which created a sensation of chaos.

It was difficult at first for me to focus on any one thing, as my attention felt pulled in all directions. The garish black and white chessboard-patterned floor created the impression of movement, making concentration even more difficult. This was certainly no ordinary Catholic Church, no peaceful place of prayer.

When I was finally able to focus my attention, I saw that the church contained several odd life-size statues. The most prominent was one of Saint Mary Magdalene, the patron saint of the church. She was depicted as holding in one hand a peculiar-looking cross made from the branches of a tree, and in the other hand a more traditional unguent jar.

The most unusual feature of the statue was a macabre human skull that rested on an open book at her feet. It was the strangest statue I had ever seen.

There were also statues of Joseph and the Virgin Mary, either one of which, if presented alone, would not have looked strange. But in this church, Joseph and Mary were turned towards one another, each holding a baby in their arms. This unusual arrangement seemed to suggest that there had been more than one child between them. Why, I wondered, had these statues been arranged this way?

In addition, there was an elaborate statue of four angels facing in the four directions. They were holding up a saint whom I immediately recognized as one of my grandmother's favorites, St. Anthony, the patron saint of lost objects. Whenever any of my sisters or brothers had lost something, we'd been instructed by my grandmother to pray to Saint Anthony. Amazingly, it always seemed our lost objects had turned up!

Was this Father Saunière's way of hinting that he had actually found something that had been lost, as Alicia had suggested? And if so, what was it? If it had just been a financial treasure, why would he have designed this bizarre church?

Among the other statues was one of John the Baptist pouring water on the head of a kneeling Jesus. This statue would have been traditional if John the Baptist's eyes had been looking at Jesus. Instead, they were locked across the checkerboard floor in a very direct and obvious exchange with the devil, which held the water font on his head.

I looked up, bewildered, at Alicia. Wordlessly, she once again simply shrugged her shoulders, leading the way to the next exhibit.

We arrived at a statue of a different St. Anthony in the church. "He's St. Anthony the Hermit," explained Alicia. "He lived at the time of Constantine and was known for ceaselessly fighting with devils. His feast day, January 17th, is very important here at Rennes le Château. A ray of sunlight actually passes through that stained glass window," she said, pointing behind the statue, "and illuminates it on that exact day every year.

"January 17th is also the date when Father Saunière had a stroke from which he never recovered, the day his housekeeper died and the same day that the last descendent of the village's noble family, said to be a guardian of a great secret, died. It was also, oddly enough, the day the god, Osiris, was celebrated in ancient Egypt.

Was the date of January 17th just an odd coincidence? And where in the world did Alicia get all this information? The woman was a veritable encyclopedia of historical information, I thought.

"Back up a minute," I told her. "Do you mean it's possible to design a window to capture light on a specific day of the year?" I was recalling the amazing violet light in the Chapel of Saint Mary at the Cathar château of Peyrepertuse.

"Absolutely," Alicia replied. "The manipulation of light was a science practiced by the ancient mystery schools. Many of the Cathar châteaux have such features. Do you remember in the Gospel of Saint John, the Cathar's favorite gospel, that Jesus says, 'I am the Light, the Truth and the Way'? The Cathar considered all light to be divine, not of the material world."

What did she mean by ancient mystery schools? I let the question go for now, and continued to explore the church. I discovered that even the most familiar ecclesiastical decorations had been distorted. For example, the familiar Stations of the Cross were arranged in the opposite direction and contained strange additions.

The station representing Pontius Pilate washing his hands, which at first looked traditional, upon closer inspection revealed Pilate to be wearing a veil, making him almost indistinguishable from a woman. Another station that initially looked like the familiar depiction of Jesus carrying the cross along Calvary displayed a person in the crowd dressed in a tartan kilt, hardly the garb of the first century Jerusalem population!

Station ten, which traditionally represents the Roman soldier's rolling dice for Jesus' clothing, also at first looked normal. But on closer inspection, one of the two die shows both a three and a four on its face. The other shows a five.

Five, Alicia pointed out, is the sacred number of perfection, according to the ancient Pythagorean mystery school. Three and four together equal seven, the number symbolizing the materialization of the perfect.

What does Pythagoras have to do with Rennes le Château? I asked myself. Doesn't he belong in a mathematics class, not a church?

Beneath the altar was a bas-relief of Mary Magdalene kneeling in a grotto before another cross formed by two branches. "Look at the difference in those branches," Alicia now pointed out. "One of the branches making up the cross is obviously alive and flourishing, while the other is withered and clearly dead. And see her fingers, the interesting way they're crossed? That's supposed to have significant symbolic meaning. Botticelli, the famous Renaissance painter, often depicted women with their fingers crossed in that same way."

"Who's that?" I asked, pointing to a statue of a man with a dog. The man had a bloody wound on his leg and seemed to be feeding the dog a large, spherical stone.

"That's St. Roch," replied Alicia. "He's a French saint believed to have had some connection to the Merovingians. Perhaps he was an heir himself. The stone he's feeding to the dog is said to represent the alchemical Philosopher's Stone, and the blood on his thigh is said to be related to the Fisher King from the Grail story."

The Philosopher's Stone? The Fisher King? The Grail Story? I remembered the bewildering Grail representations in the cave at the Cathar château of Montreal de Sol. I remembered also the many references I found referring to Montségur as The Grail Castle.

"You know, I'm beginning to feel a bit overwhelmed," I told Alicia. "This place is so bizarre, it's like being in the fun house at a country fair."

Alicia pointed to the door and I breathed a deep sigh of relief once we were outside again. "Let's go over there," Alicia suggested, pointing in the direction of a garden directly adjacent to the church. We entered the garden and silently walked among the flowers and the rocks with which Saunière had decorated it. The sunshine, the soft earth beneath my feet and the freshness of the air upon my skin had an immediate calming effect.

The grotto felt cool and very quiet. Alicia walked on, but I felt exhausted from all the confusion of the church, and sat down to collect my thoughts beneath a huge ancient hemlock tree. A cuckoo called in the distance.

Was there any possibility, I wondered, that Father Saunière's church decorations had really been designed to communicate a secret he had discovered? Was it possible that he had been speaking in some kind of code? Why couldn't he just have come straight out with it?

But the garden was so peaceful and relaxing I couldn't quite keep my thoughts focused. After awhile I grew tired of thinking about it all and just leaned my head back against the trunk of the tree.

I closed my eyes, and the next thing I remember is slowly becoming aware of what sounded like a clock, loudly, rhythmically ticking. Where is that sound coming from? I asked myself as I opened my eyes and looked around.

But the garden was completely silent. Convincing myself that I'd imagined what I'd heard, I leaned my head back against the trunk of the tree. Not long afterward, however, the sound began again and this time the loud ticking began to frighten me.

I stood up so fast I almost fainted. I could still hear clearly what sounded like a clock, loudly, rhythmically, menacingly ticking,

Where's Alicia? I wondered, beginning to panic. Turning around to look for her, I found myself facing an iron gate, above which sat a large sculpted skull and crossbones. The skull's mouth was open and revealed a wide, ominous leer.

My first reaction was to run, but then I saw Alicia looking through a pile of rocks on the other side of the garden. She glanced up when she saw me. "What's happened to you? Are you OK?" she called. "You look as if you've just seen a ghost!"

I stalled, and then pointed to the morbid skull and crossbones. "Ugly, isn't it?" asked Alicia. "Scary, too. There are twenty-two teeth in that mouth, another very popular number here at Rennes le Château. There are also twenty-two stairs in the *Tour Magdala* and 22 letters in the Hebrew alphabet. Maybe it's just a coincidence. But maybe not."

"Mary Magdalene's feast day is July 22," I interrupted, suddenly recalling this fact. "And isn't that the day the crusade against the Cathar began?"

"That's right," Alicia nodded. "Behind that gate with the nasty skull and crossbones is the village cemetery. It's the final resting place of generations of village inhabitants, including Saunière, his housekeeper, and Marie de Blanchefort, the last descendant of the village's most illustrious family."

"Who?" I asked, still trying to shake the memory of the ticking sound and at the same time to assimilate the new name.

"According to a widely believed story," Alicia began, "In the late eighteenth century, Marie de Blanchefort was near death and without any living descendants. On her deathbed, she made to the village priest, Father Saunière's predecessor, a mysterious secret confession, and gave him some historical documents belonging to her ancestors. Before her last breath, Marie made the priest promise that he would pass along the secret she had revealed, as well as the documents, to someone who would preserve them and continue to pass them on."

Apparently, Alicia told me, some researchers believed that one of the mysterious documents was a genealogy that confirmed that a Merovingian heir had actually survived the Church's attempts to wipe out the royal blood line, and that he had been brought to Rennes le Château for safekeeping, where he lived out his life in peace. The secret genealogy also supposedly revealed the identity of the royal bloodlines surprising origins."

"What do you mean by *the dynasty's surprising origins*?" I demanded. "Surprising how?"

"I have no idea," replied Alicia, "It's just another one of Rennes le Château's many mysteries."

"And what was a dying woman doing with a genealogy of the Merovingians? Was she herself a descendent?"

"Perhaps," replied Alicia. "Or she married into the family. In any case historical records confirm that the Blanchefort family was also involved in the negotiation of the fifteen day truce before the fire at Montségur and also the rescue of the Cathar treasure from the mountain. "

While I tried to make sense of this new information, Alicia suggested that we visit the village museum. "Let's go see what we can find out—that is, if it's open. Every time I've been here before, it's been closed. But maybe today we'll get lucky."

We followed the signs to the museum, quickly arriving before a small building. We found the museum open but haphazardly arranged, with a wide assortment of poorly organized information pertaining to the Abbe Bérenger Saunière and his mysterious domain.

On display were Saunière's personal effects. There were newspaper clippings, letters, and the priest's account books, all of which clearly reflected his sudden increase in wealth. There were also photographs showing Saunière with his pretty young housekeeper, Marie, dressed in the latest Paris fashions, entertaining celebrated guests from all over the world, including members of the royal Hapsburg court.

Also on exhibit was an array of strange documents referring to an erased tombstone in the village cemetery and to an ancient funerary monument near the Cathar village of Arques.

Back in the car, we drove along silently. Eventually I dozed a bit, and in no time at all, we were home.

"Oh, there's one more thing I nearly forgot to tell you," Alicia said as we pulled into my driveway, suddenly becoming the historian again. "Do you remember the carved white stone in the museum?"

I turned to Alicia. "You know, I think I've absorbed enough for today. How about you?"

"Right," said Alicia, "That's enough for me, too."

Alicia seemed to have no problem with my sudden need for a break from Cathar history. "Listen, luv, I'm off to England tomorrow. I'll ring you when I return," she replied.

"I know I'll have a lot to ask you once I've had a chance to think about Rennes le Château," I promised her, smiling apologetically. Alicia laughed, waved, and drove off.

There were so many questions. Deathbed secrets, ancient gene-alogies, strange symbols and magical numbers, encrypted messages, lost treasure...

Rennes le Château seemed a loonybin of impenetrable riddles. And why had the church been dedicated to Mary Magdalene? Why were there so many statues of her? Why had the beautiful tower been given her name?? And what was that ticking sound I had heard?

CHAPTER TWELVE

The Templar Seal

The spiritual element is not a silent partner in the business of life,
but demands active participation in the growth and transformation
of the individual. Unlike the mind-emotion complex,
the pneumatic component does not express itself in words or
in ordinary feelings. Dreams, visions and altered states
of consciousness and what Jung called synchronistic experiences are
the most important avenues for the symbolic communications.

Stephan A. Hoeller, *The Gnostic Jung*

ABOUT A WEEK AFTER MY VISIT to Rennes le Château, I
awoke suddenly from a dream, terrified and short of breath. "What were
you dreaming?" Bill asked later, passing me a *croissant* as we sat together
in our garden eating breakfast.

"It was very confusing," I said. "The only part I can remember clearly is
that I was on a horse. I was riding frantically through the night, carrying
a child. I was terrified that I was being chased by someone—I kept hearing
thundering hoof beats behind me. I knew that my pursuer had evil designs
on the child in my arms. I never actually saw the child's face—I don't even
know if it was a boy or a girl. But I clearly remember the smell of its hair,
and thinking that no matter what, I couldn't let anything happen to it."

"Well, don't leave me hanging," asked Bill. "Did you get to your destination safely?"

"I don't know," I replied. "I woke up before I ever arrived." Then, I suddenly remembered something else. "Oh, yes, I was dressed completely in white, with an equal-armed red cross emblazoned across my chest."

Bill leaned over and kissed me on the cheek. "Well, there's nothing strange about that, Janet. You love white. In fact, you have more white clothes in your closet than anyone I know. Anyway, you're safe now, sweetie," he said reassuringly, "and it's a beautiful day. Hey, did you see the white calla lilies blooming in the front yard? I think all this Cathar stuff is really starting to get to you. Maybe you should give it a break for awhile."

Despite Bill's attempts to divert my attention that morning, the anxiety from my dream lingered on into the afternoon. I just couldn't shake it off. As I made the beds, watered the plants, cleaned up the breakfast dishes, and checked out the blooming calla lilies in the front yard, I continued to feel a strange fear of being hunted down.

Late in the morning, after the kids and Bill had left the house for the day, I curled up on the couch with a book, still weary from my restless night. No sooner had I closed my eyes than the buzzer on the gate rang. Startled, I rose to my feet and began moving toward the sound. As I opened the front door, sunlight spilled into the dark foyer and spread across the terra cotta tiles carrying with it the perfume from the front yard's summer flowers. Peering out into the thick green foliage that bordered the path to the wrought iron gate, I was both surprised and delighted to find Chris' smiling face looking back at me.

I hurried along through the trees towards her as she called out a greeting. "I am back from England and I've just been to the market in Cugnaux. I decided on a whim to pop in and see if you were home," she said.

"I'm so glad you're here," I replied, leading her through the house and out into the garden. "To tell you the truth," I began, "I'm in the middle of trying to shake off a bad dream I had last night."

"What did you dream?" she asked.

When I'd finished describing it, much to my astonishment, Chris laughed. "What? What's so funny?" I asked, feeling slightly offended.

"I'm not laughing at you," she assured me. "It's just that your dreams are so unusual. Alicia told me she was going to take you to Rennes le Château while I was away. It sounds like you went! "

"Why? " I asked, suddenly alert. "What does my dream have to do with Rennes le Château?" "Maybe," she offered, "your dream is related to the *Templar Stone* at Rennes le Château. Maybe the frantic ride on the horse while carrying a child..."

"Wait a second," I stopped her. "You're going too fast for me. What are you talking about?"

"You know," said Chris, "that carved white stone that shows the two Templar Knights riding on the one horse. I'm pretty sure it's upstairs in the museum on one of the back walls. It's called the *Dalle des Chevaliers*, I believe. At one time the stone marked a crypt inside the church where at least one Merovingian is thought to have been buried."

"I don't remember anything resembling what you're describing," I said. Nor did I remember that a Merovingian had been buried in the church. "Maybe I saw the stone you're referring to, and then forgot about it. I must have. Oh, and in the dream I was wearing all white. Does that mean anything to you?" I asked her.

"I know the Knights Templar wore all white, "she recalled.

"All white with an equal-armed red cross emblazoned across the front?"

"Exactly," replied Chris.

"OK. So who were the Templar Knights?" I asked, feeling a bit foolish.

"You mean you've never heard of them?" Chris stared at me wonderingly. "They're quite famous throughout Europe." She considered my origins then, and said comfortingly, "Well, maybe no one learns about them in America. I had to do a research report on them in secondary school and I've been fascinated with them ever since, as many people are. Their history is all tied up with Rennes le Château and with the Merovingians and the Cathar. In fact, an early grand master of the Templar was an ancestor of the woman from Rennes le Château who passed on the genealogies and secrets to the village priest."

"Marie de Blanchefort?" I asked.

"You remembered her name! I'm impressed!" said Chris, regarding me with affection.

"So you're telling me that not just the Cathar and the Merovingians were connected to Rennes le Château, but also an order of medieval knights who dressed all in white?"

"Right," confirmed Chris. "It does at times seem that all roads lead to Rennes le Château. The Templar Knights are actually rumored to have been the protectors of the Holy Grail. It's almost certain that one of their early members was the first to write down the Grail story. I think the scene on the stone in your dream was used at one point by the Knights Templar as their official seal," Chris said. "Yes, in fact I'm quite sure they used that scene as one of their seals."

"So who were the Templar?" I asked impatiently.

"They were best known as the white knights who defended the Holy Lands during the crusades. They were founded in the twelfth century and grew to become the best trained, best equipped and most professional military force in the Western world. They actually were warrior monks. They took vows of poverty, chastity and obedience, and in the early years of their founding, lived monastically. The order was under the leadership of St. Bernard. Have you heard about him?" she asked.

"I've certainly known his name since I was a child. I had a holy card with his picture on it. What I'm finding out, though, is that we Catholics don't know much of anything about real history. There was a picture of him in one of my Cathar books and I do recall reading that he initially defended them," I replied.

"That's right," Chris acknowledged. "When he was alive, which was before the Cathar crusade, he spoke of the Cathar with the highest respect. Bernard was a Cistercian monk committed to a simple life of austerity, but he was also one of the most influential individuals in medieval Christendom. His advice was sought throughout the Western world by both popes and kings. I think the Templar were actually the military arm of Bernard's Cistercian monastic order."

"A monastic order needed a military arm?" I asked.

Chris shrugged. "There are actually quite a few questions about the Templar. For example, during the first decade of their existence, their ranks consisted of only nine knights. Their official *raison d'être* was to provide protection to Western Christian pilgrims in the Holy Lands, but with only nine knights in their ranks, they could hardly have carried out this role effectively. So it's widely assumed that from their inception, the knights were involved in some clandestine endeavor.

"During their early years, they supposedly lived in Jerusalem near the ancient temple of Solomon. Some historians believe that they were actually in the Holy Lands on a secret excavation mission. After nine years, presumably having retrieved what they had come for, they returned from the Holy Lands to Europe and were received by St. Bernard with great celebration,

"You're not going to tell me that the Templar Knights were also involved with a secret treasure, are you?" I interrupted.

"I'm afraid so. In the years following their return to Europe they became fabulously wealthy," continued Chris. "After the Crusades, they built a huge shipping empire and became not only the financiers of the Pope and the European nobility, but their friends and counselors. I've heard there's even a Templar signature on the Magna Carta and that Templar maps were used by Columbus on his famous voyage of 1492."

My head was swimming with all this information. And once again, I was feeling like I was the only person in the world never having heard a word about a group of important players in world history.

"Unfortunately for the Templar," Chris continued, "in the fourteenth century, long after St. Bernard was around to protect them, they ran into a little trouble with the Church and were arrested as heretics. Soon after, the order was disbanded."

"What happened?" I asked. "I thought you said they fought for the Church during the crusades?"

"It's quite a mystery. We do know that on Friday, October 13th, 1307, the king of France ordered the arrest of all the Templar in his domain. The date of the Templar's arrest is actually how Friday the 13th became known as a day of bad luck. After their arrest, the Templar all over Europe were turned over to the Inquisition and subjected to torture, executions and censure of their order. In 1314, the Templar's last grand master, Jacques de Molay, was burnt at the stake in Paris for heresy."

"What crimes were the Templar charged with?" I asked, fascinated.

"Heresy is all I know," admitted Chris. "Alicia may know more. But after their arrest, the Church, as it did with all of its Inquisition victims including the Cathar, attempted to totally erase any trace of the group from the pages of history. I have read that the Templar refused to worship the crucifix and worshiped a head or skull instead."

"A human skull?" I asked. "You mean like the one at Mary Magdalene's feet at Rennes le Château? And isn't there another at her side in the bas-relief on the front altar? Oh, and there's also that awful skull and crossbones over the gate of the graveyard."

"Right," said Chris. "The Knights Templar are definitely all tied up in the mysteries of Rennes le Château. The skull and crossbones was flown from the masts of their ships. Then, the pirates of the high seas took the flag over after the Templar had officially been disbanded. And now it is used as a symbol for poison.

"The knights in fact, became the subjects of many fabulous myths and legends throughout Europe after their demise," Chris continued. "The Grail Romances portray them as having been the protectors of great mystical secrets. As an added note, it's very possible that both Bernard's monastic order and the Templar Knights were dedicated to Mary Magdalene."

"Oh, great!" Chris suddenly exclaimed, glancing down at her watch. "Look at the time! I've got to go! Michael's bringing business associates home for dinner tonight. I'll call you soon," she promised and then hurried out the door and down the path.

"But wait a minute! I have a million questions!" I protested.

"Sorry, but I do have to go," called back Chris. "I'll phone you next week—promise!"

CHAPTER THIRTEEN

At The Night Market

She is the Shekinah, the compassionate presence of God in exile.
She may also be seen as a paradigm for the Grail—
the vessel of honor which stands as a covenant for all of God's
mercy and richness, a presence to be sought,
a love which prompts mystics to journey in perpetual quest
until union or realization is achieved and the world redeemed at last.

John Matthews, *The Grail Tradition*

I DIDN'T HEAR FROM either Chris or Alicia the following week, but spent a great deal of time on my computer reading everything I could find on the Knights Templar. In 1214, I learned, the order, known in the Middle Ages as the *Warriors of God*, was officially dissolved. Its last Grand Master, Jacques de Molay, still protesting the Templar's innocence, had been burned at the stake for heresy over a slow fire in Paris.

None of what I read, however, explained the exact nature of the Templar's supposed heresy, nor did it explain the mysteries in the Templar's history. What was the original reason for their founding? Had they unearthed some treasure in the Holy Lands? Why had they been arrested? What did the Templar have to do with the Blanchefort woman at Rennes le Château who seemed to be connected to the royal Merovingians, and the Cathar of Montségur? And what about their dedication to Mary Magdalene?

None of the Templar's own documents or records had ever been recovered, and even their immense wealth, which the king of France had intended to seize to replenish his own depleted coffers, had mysteriously disappeared. Their awesome shipping fleet, which had included at least 18 galleys, had simply vanished. It staggered the mind that an entire shipping fleet with all its cargo could just completely disappear, especially with the King of France looking for it. One article I read suggested that the Templar's stated objective—to protect the routes to the Holy Lands—had never been intended to be taken literally. I couldn't even fathom what this could mean.

Finding little to add to what Chris had already told me about the Knights Templar, I turned my attention to another enigma that kept popping up: the Holy Grail. The Knights Templar were said to have been its guardians and Montségur to have been its castle. There had also been several mentions of the Grail at Rennes le Château.

The available literature on the Grail was voluminous but fascinating. From what I was able to gather, the mythic quest for the Grail had most likely originated as an oral tradition with the Celts, the ancient people of the British Isles whose migration brought them into France, Germany and Spain. The earliest known Grail text, *Le Conte del Graal*, I learned, was written in 1170 by a French poet, alleged to have been either an associate of the Templar or a knight himself. Some time between the late twelfth century and the early thirteenth century, St. Bernard, the spiritual founder of the Templar, and his Cistercian monks at the monastery of Clairvaux had taken over as the principal Grail storytellers.

I couldn't help but notice that the influence of the pious St. Bernard in the medieval world was extraordinary. He seemed to have been almost everywhere.

While it would probably take years of research to even begin to understand the Grail tradition, from what I could make out, the stories all chronicled a knight's quest to find the Holy Grail. In each version, the knights who set out on the quest were given a series of symbolic tests and trials. For those who were successful, a final initiation was presented.

The tales were told in a complex symbolic language involving dreams, enchantments and magic of all sorts and the knights had names like Galahad, Gawain, Bors, Lancelot and Perceval. The major themes of the stories involve such characters as a king with a wound that will not heal and challenges such as restoring a *Wasteland*.

The Wounded King reminded me of the statue of the saint with a pierced bloody thigh in the church at Rennes le Château.

Alicia had said the saint was related to the Grail. Was he the *Wounded King*? What was meant by the *Wasteland*?

The sought-after object in all of the Grail stories is the Grail itself, which takes on many mysterious forms, depending on its story's author. It has been represented as a magic cauldron, a precious stone, usually an emerald that has fallen from heaven, a wondrous dish, a cup used to catch the blood of the dieing Jesus and a severed human head. The head reminded me of the Mary Magdalene statues at Rennes le Château. In whatever its form the Grail is sought for its miraculous capacities to heal, give forth rich foods, bestow rare favors upon its owner and provide entry into the mysterious world of spirit and pure light.

In certain of the Grail stories, I found distinct allusions to its feminine nature. I also found obscure suggestions of a secret lineage of Grail Kings or a Grail Family, *known only to the angels.*

This human succession of kings was said to be responsible for guarding the Grail and passing down its secrets to each one of their successors. Was this concept of a Grail Family meant to be allegorical, I wondered? I had heard the Cathar described as guardians of the Grail and the Templar as the Grail's protectors. Somehow, the idea of a lineage of Grail Kings reminded me of the Merovingians.

Further in my Grail research, I found references to a Grail Temple or Grail Castle where its secrets could be kept safe until, *mankind was deemed ready to be told of its existence, shown its miraculous powers and ready to go in search of what it represented.* Was Montségur the Grail Castle?

After learning all that I had about the mystical Quest for the Grail, I couldn't help wonder why I had never heard anything about it before? Of course I should have known the answer by now.

As I read on, I learned that the Grail Tradition, long after Bernard had been around to protect it, had been outlawed by the Church. According to what I learned, the Grail Quest was alleged to perpetuate *a secret esoteric doctrine of antiquity* that described an independent search for mystical awakening. It offered a path completely outside the confines of the Church. For this reason, the Grail Quest was ultimately deemed a heresy and those involved met their end in the fires of the Inquisition.

Again I had the sensation that I was assembling a large and frustrating jigsaw puzzle. Somehow I knew that all these pieces had to fit together. I just couldn't see exactly how. It seemed impossible that only coincidence connected all of this together.

On Friday afternoon, Chris surprised me with a telephone call, asking if Bill and I would like to accompany her and Michael that evening to a night market. While I had never been to a night market and wasn't even sure what one was, I couldn't wait to talk to Chris again and I was definitely needing a change of scene. So without even waiting to consult Bill, I agreed that we'd join them.

Later that evening, we met Chris and Michael at their home. After a convivial glass of wine together, the four of us headed out to experience the night market.

Michael drove northwest away from Toulouse, and in less than twenty minutes we were surrounded by the lush, rolling hills of Cathar country, still flowering with the summer's harvest. Ripening beneath the heat of the summer sun, in every direction, were grapes, garlic and giant sunflowers, their heads now hanging low with the weight of their seeds.

As we traveled past the rich fields, I felt the names, dates and upsetting ideas that had disturbed me for the past few months take flight. I relaxed into Bill's arm, which rested comfortably upon my shoulder, and gazed out of the open window of the car. Once in awhile we passed an isolated stone farm building with a barnyard of geese.

"It's *foie gras* country," Michael explained. For awhile, we drove along in comfortable silence, just drinking in the scenery.

"Did you know," asked Michael, interrupting the silence, "that hundreds of years ago these fields were all planted in *pastel*, the source of blue dye that brought the Toulousians of the Middle Ages their great wealth? I once heard," he continued, "that the Cathar weavers used the *pastel* plant to color their cloth."

I listened and nodded my appreciation for the information, then happily turned my attention once again to the silence.

After driving for almost an hour, we came to the edge of a village and Michael brought the car to a stop. "OK, this is it!" he announced, smiling broadly. This is what? Bill and I both wondered silently.

Michael and Chris led us down a narrow street, and as we turned a corner we found the answer to our question. The sights, sounds and smells of the night market immediately seized our senses. Delicious aromas of cooking food danced on the warm night air and instantly whet our appetites.

Magret de Canard and French-cut potatoes were frying on enormous grills, spitting their delicious juices into the light wind. Garlic soup steamed in huge metal vats and pots, that appeared to have been cooking for days, simmered the blend of white beans, pork fat, sausage and duck, known in the south of France as *cassoulet*.

As we entered the village square, we found that the cooking food was encircled with a lavish display of the year's harvest. Atop wooden boxes were stacked perfectly ripened peaches, grapes, apples, eggplants, tomatoes and shining peppers of yellow, red and green still warm from the day's sun.

The village *fromagers* flaunted fat rounds of pale yellow, white, and delicate green hued spheres of cheeses, while the *boulangers* proudly exhibited their crispy *baguettes*, golden flutes and huge loaves of dark, crusted breads in tidy mounds. There were bottles of Armagnac, the region's fiery, aged elixir, displayed for sampling, and wines from the village cooperatives flowed from dark wooden kegs overflowing into glasses and splashing on the ground.

Having worked up a healthy appetite, we began making our selections from the enormous possibilities. With our plates overflowing with all that we could manage to carry, we chose a bottle of wine and then found a place to sit at one of the many white paper-covered wooden tables set up around a band playing old French songs. After having consumed their fill, Michael and Bill excused themselves and headed toward the Armagnac tasting table.

At first, because of the noise of the celebration, talking amongst ourselves had been almost impossible. But now, adjusted to the uproar, Chris and I relaxed beneath the stars, which had just come out in the early evening sky.

I told Chris all I had learned about the Holy Grail during the past week. Her response led me to believe that she'd been waiting all evening, as had I, to get to this moment where we could discuss our shared passion.

"It's beginning to look to me as if the Templar, the Grail, the mysterious Cathar, the royal Merovingians, and the enigmatic village of Rennes le Château, are all tied together," I said. "Do you think it's possible?"

It felt like a tremendous relief to be able to speak to someone who actually found this history as fascinating as I did.

"I came across something interesting this week," Chris said excitedly. "I read that one of the problems the Templar had with the Church was their relationship with the number five and the pentagram. For some reason, the Church associated the number and shape with the Devil! I also learned that there are some caves in the Ariège River Valley said to have been hiding places for the Cathar, with pentagrams painted on the walls."

"That's fascinating!" I agreed. "And did you know there's also a prominent number five in one of the odd Stations of the Cross at Rennes le Château? Alicia told me the number five was used as a symbol for *perfection* by the ancient Pythagorean mystery school."

Mutually absorbed in our conversation, we grew increasingly oblivious to the pleasant commotion of the night market around us. As a result, we were both surprised when a woman sitting next to Chris leaned over and touched her arm. Chris almost jumped from her seat in surprise.

"Excuse me," the woman said in perfect English, "but I couldn't help overhearing your fascinating discussion."

It was always surprising to hear English spoken in the Languedoc but in these surroundings and in the midst of our specific conversation it was a shock. As Chris and I both turned to face her, it was immediately clear to us that the woman was not a resident of the village. Handsomely dressed and sporting a fashionable haircut, she sat beside an attractive man wearing a dark suit, along with two young children who looked as if they had been freshly scrubbed for the evening's festivities.

I was taken aback, not only by the interruption, but by the fact that we hadn't noticed this family, so unlike the rest of the crowd, sooner.

Without realizing how startled Chris and I had been, the woman continued to speak. She introduced herself as a biblical scholar from Oxford traveling through France with her husband and children. "We're on our way to visit friends who live south of Toulouse," she said. "We got off the *autoroute* to find something to eat. By pure chance we happened upon this wonderful little festival. Isn't it delightful?" she asked.

"Yes, we're having a wonderful time," Chris replied with a smile.

The woman chattered on merrily. "I'm working on a research project right now that involves Mary Magdalene. I think I heard you mention the name of a village that's considered one of the oldest sites of the cultic worship of the Magdalene in France."

Chris and I both stared back at her, dumbfounded.

"Didn't I hear you refer to a village named Rennes Le Château?" she asked, unsure why we weren't responding.

"Yes," I said, finally finding my tongue. "But I've never heard it referred to as a site of 'cultic Mary Magdalene worship.' Have you?" I asked turning to Chris. Chris shook her head.

"I've just been to Rennes le Château for the first time, and Chris has been there several times," I continued. "We're absolutely fascinated by the place, but we haven't been able to make much sense of it."

"Well," said the woman. "My ideas are not what you would call orthodox and I wouldn't want to offend you in any way..."

"No, please go on," we both urged her. In fact, wild horses couldn't have torn us away.

Reassured, she continued, "The Mary Magdalene of my research is definitely not the same person the Church defined as the *penitent whore*. Are you familiar with the legend of the Magdalene's immigration to France?" she asked.

Chris and I both shook our heads.

"She came to France accompanied by a small group of friends, seeking safety from the Roman authorities right after the crucifixion of her husband. Are you aware," she continued, "that many Biblical scholars believe that the Magdalene was not only the wife of Jesus and the mother of his children, but the matriarch of what later became the French Merovingian dynasty?"

"What?" exclaimed Chris, speaking for both of us.

"The origin of the name Merovingian actually comes from a French word with two meanings," the woman explained. "*Mer* means mother, and also sea. The Magdalene was the mother who came from across the sea. You've probably heard the legend of the Merovingian's descent from a sea creature?" she asked. "This is its basis." At this point she again paused, waiting for our response.

"Wasn't the sea creature called something like a *quinotaur*?" I asked.

"Correct," she replied. "That refers, of course, to the Merovingians' relationship with the spiritual number five, the symbol of *perfection*."

"Please go on," said Chris, looking at me, her eyes wide with disbelief.

"I've heard," said the woman, "that there is an ancient church in this vicinity that still has windows displaying the Star of David, the lineage of the Magdalene's children."

I knew at once that she was referring to the windows in the church at Alet-les-Bains.

The woman stopped to sip her wine as we momentarily sat speechless. I thought of many things to say but instead remained silent and waited for her to go on.

"But you don't actually mean you believe Mary Magdalene was the wife of Jesus, and that they had children together?" Chris asked incredulously.

"That's exactly what I'm saying," replied the woman. "Apocryphal sources confirm it conclusively. Before immigrating to France, Mary Magdalene was a spiritual leader of high authority in the Jerusalem community. Later she was referred to as the *Watchtower* for her role in watching over the tradition of Jesus

"Are you also saying," I asked, "that Mary Magdalene moved to France, and that her descendants were the royal French Merovingians?"

The woman nodded her head. She then turned her attention to the food on the plate in front of her. As she ate, she was silent, and I took the break in the conversation as an opportunity to digest this explosive theory of hers.

I found myself both shocked and somehow outraged. As much as I had learned about the Church's lies, its cover-ups, its Holy War against the gentle Cathar, I still wasn't ready to accept what I had just heard. The implications of her statements were astounding. Mary Magdalene, the wife of Jesus, mother of his children, a teacher of high authority in the Jerusalem community, the watchtower of the teachings, a Merovingian?

But if it were true... As my thoughts alternated between outright rejection and acceptance of what the woman was saying, I suddenly recalled the experience I'd had while resting in Saunière's garden on my visit to Rennes Le Château. I remembered clearly hearing the sound of a clock ticking. The watchtower? I silently asked myself.

The woman interrupted my reflections when she began to speak again. "It's certainly no secret," she said, "that the early Christian Fathers despised women. And Mary Magdalene was no ordinary woman—she was a woman who posed a very serious threat to the Church. She not only was the wife of Jesus and mother of the descendants of the Biblical Line of David, but she was associated with an ancient body of mystical teachings long represented by the Divine Feminine, a tradition strictly forbidden by the Council of Nicea.

"The Church had to get rid of her to prevent a possible challenge to the Pope's authority and to all that he stood for. So they declared her a prostitute, the most degrading title that could be given to a woman and the most foolproof way to relegate a woman to insignificance."

"So you're saying that Mary Magdalene really wasn't a whore?" asked Chris, not mincing her words.

"Good God, no! Of course not! Calling a woman a whore is an age-old means of discrediting her. It works every time. There isn't a shred of evidence to support such a thing. This was a total fabrication of the Church Fathers. In fact," she laughed cynically, "the Church Fathers went so far as to associate the color red, which Mary Magdalene often wore to denote her high spiritual rank in the community, with sinful women! Later the Merovingians also associated themselves with the color red in honor of their sacred royal blood."

"Back up a minute," I urged. "Are you implying that the Merovingian dynasty was actually the biblical Line of David."

"I am," she replied confidently. "And by the way, my name is Louise," she said as she held out her hand to us. Then, not waiting for us to introduce ourselves, she continued.

"Jesus was the heir to the Royal House of David. It naturally follows that his children continued the bloodline. In addition to perpetuating the royal bloodline, the Merovingians also preserved the ancient spiritual traditions and initiate's path that had been associated with the Line of David since Abraham, or possibly even earlier. Actually, the Old Testament emphasizes that Abraham and Jesus were initiated by Melchizedek, an ancient priest king. Melchizedek is believed to have received his knowledge from Egypt and the ancient Egyptians referred to the initiatic path as a legacy handed down to them."

"This is quite an amazing perspective you're presenting," interrupted Chris, shooting me a companionably skeptical look.

"Well," said Louise, "to even begin to comprehend the mysteries of Rennes le Château, you must understand that while the Church Fathers could successfully suppress the Magdalene's true identity throughout most of Western Christendom, they had one big problem: that problem was France.

"Here, where Mary Magdalene had lived and died, her reputation was well established and eluded the Church's manipulative grasp. Despite all the Church's efforts, which were often extreme, the people of France held tenaciously to their perception of The Magdalene. For them, she was the chief disciple of Christ and the principal protector of the mystical spiritual traditions that he represented. The Orthodox Church was something altogether different, a total corruption."

I shot a look at Chris, but she was too deeply engrossed in what Louise was saying to notice.

"Rennes Le Château is just one of the important sites where she was worshiped against the wishes of the Church," Louise continued. "France refused to be controlled by the Church regarding Mary Magdalene, and this eventually became a major problem for the ecclesiastic authorities in Rome. You must have heard of the Cathar?"

My heart began to race just hearing her say the word. What connection would she make between the Cathar, the Merovingians, and The Magdalene?

"Yes," said Chris, "we do know a bit about the Cathar."

"Suffice it to say, the Cathar were well aware of Mary Magdalene's true identity. They were initiates themselves of the pure tradition and many of their members were of the royal bloodline. Did you know that the crusade against the Cathar was actually launched on Mary's feast day? This is no coincidence. The biggest problem in all of it now, as far as I am concerned," continued Louise, "is that except for places like Rennes le Château, the rich and ancient spiritual traditions of which Jesus and Mary Magdalene were initiates appear to have been almost completely lost. The white knights protected the Grail and its Family only for as long as they were able to."

As Louise paused to sip her wine again, suddenly the sky opened up and sheets of rain began pouring down on the night market. The band, sheltered under a pavilion, continued to play while everyone else scattered to find cover. As thunder crashed and lightning split the darkness, Louise grabbed her children and, along with her husband, dashed into the night.

Chris and I just stood there, unable to move. We allowed the rain to soak us as we watched the woman and her family take flight. The next moment, Louise was gone, swallowed up forever by the rain and darkness.

Chris and I, completely soaked, grabbed each other's hands and ran toward where we had parked the car. There, we found Michael and Bill waiting for us, as we had hoped. I volunteered to drive as both men admitted to feeling the strong effects of the Armagnac. The rain continued to fall heavily, making visibility challenging.

But even more hazardous than the rain were the droves of frogs leaping across the road in front of us. I had never seen anything like it. It was as if some enormous frog festival had been interrupted by the weather. After awhile, as the frogs continued to leap across the road and I continued to swerve, Chris started laughing. I soon joined her. The incongruity of the procession of leaping frogs in light of all that had just happened at the night market seemed to be more than we could handle.

When we were almost home, Chris began to relate a story to us which she obviously remembered as a result of our discussion with the woman at the night market.

"My grandmother used to tell a story," began Chris, "of a beautiful dress she once had made for herself to wear on a very special occasion. When she brought the dress home to show to her family, her father suddenly grabbed it from her hands and threw it into the fire. As my shocked grandmother tearfully watched her beautiful dress destroyed in the flames, her father had shouted at her angrily, 'I will buy you another, but no daughter of mine will ever shame this family by wearing a red dress!'

"My grandmother had been horrified," said Chris. "She told the story throughout her entire life."

I understood the significance of the red dress without Chris having to elaborate. "Yes. But can you really believe that Mary Magdalene was the wife of Jesus? Can you accept the idea that they had children together?" I asked Chris.

"What the bloody hell are you saying?" asked Michael. Then, turning to Bill, he said, "They've lost their minds totally now, Bill. I don't think we'll be able to let them out of our sight again!"

CHAPTER FOURTEEN

A Case of Mistaken Identity

To begin with, her words can seem so fragile:
so easy to ignore, contradict, or argue away.
They are just a hauntingly, unfathomable voice coming through
faintly from another world with an absurd message
that spells death to everything we believe.

Peter Kingsley, *Reality*

THE MORNING AFTER MY EXPERIENCE at the night market,
I was up and sitting at the computer before dawn. I was actually surprised
that I'd been able to sleep at all.

Despite everything I'd recently learned about the Church's behavior in
regard to the Cathar, the Merovingians and the Templar Knights, despite
everything I'd learned about its deceptions and its cover-ups, I still could
not accept that Mary Magdalene, the woman represented by the Church
as the repentant prostitute, had actually been the wife of Jesus, the mother
of his children, and the highest initiate of His path.

The very idea of Jesus and Mary Magdalene as husband and wife
shook the bedrock of my fundamental belief system. It was exactly the
type of thinking the nuns and priests of my childhood had warned would
jeopardize my soul for all eternity! It was the thinking of a fanatic or of
a crazy conspiracy theorist!

But while I found myself unable to accept what Louise, the woman at the night market, had told us, I couldn't, having become aware of the Church's deceptions, outright reject her theory, either.

Now, I was sitting at the computer in the cold morning darkness, waiting for the curser to signal its readiness. I was confident that my research would prove Louise to be very, very wrong. However, if it turned out that Mary Magdalene had never really been a prostitute, but had instead been the wife of Jesus, I vowed that I would never again believe anything I had been taught about Christianity.

It did not take me long to establish that there wasn't a shred of evidence to support Mary Magdalene's reputation as a prostitute. Nevertheless, I discovered that late in the sixth century, Pope Gregory the Great, one of the most influential forces in Church history, had established as official Church canon Mary Magdalene's identity as exactly that—a repentant prostitute.

Evidently the early Christians had originally inadvertently fused Mary Magdalene with several different women from the gospel stories. However, Pope Gregory's creation of Mary as a long-haired weeping woman holding an alabaster jar in her hands and begging Jesus to forgive her sin of prostitution was, in fact, a willful misinterpretation of fact, part of a wider plot to equate feminine beauty and sexuality with sinfulness.

One respected French scholar back in the sixteenth century—also a devout Catholic—had actually tried to untangle the different women whom he believed had been fused together to create the Church's debased image of Mary Magdalene. The scholar's efforts were rewarded by the Church threatening him with immediate excommunication.

Most astonishing to me was that, according to my sources, in 1969 the Church had actually admitted its *mistake* and announced that Mary Magdalene had never been a prostitute! Yet I'd never heard anything about this. How, I wondered, had the Church made such an announcement? Was it on the evening news? Was it in the headlines of *the New York Times*? Or had the story been published in an obscure Catholic journal?

In any case, not only had I missed it, but I suspect that millions of others did, too. After all, how did one undo fourteen hundred years of *mistaken identity?*

I realized that everything I'd read so far had completely supported what the woman at the night market had said about Mary Magdalene's having been a prostitute. However, nothing even hinted that she and Jesus had been husband and wife, that she had lived in France, that she had been involved in a tradition other than that of the Catholic Church, or that her legacy had required the protection of the medieval Templar Knights. The question now arose strong and clear: if Mary Magdalene wasn't a prostitute, who was she?

Oddly, her name cannot be found in any other historical record besides the New Testament itself. One by one, I began looking through the gospels of Matthew, Mark, Luke and John for her name.

I found her first mentioned briefly in the gospel of Luke, where she was referred to as one of the women in Jesus' entourage from whom seven devils had been removed.

"Seven devils?" I repeated aloud. Now, what did that mean?

I didn't find her name again in any of the gospels until the time of the crucifixion. But from then on I found her featured as a prominent character in all four testaments. Both Mark and Matthew mentioned her by name as one of a small group who watched the Crucifixion from afar. John's gospel, which was favored by the Cathar, placed Mary Magdalene directly at the foot of the cross, along with Jesus' mother and his aunt. This certainly suggested a very close relationship, I noted. And where, I wondered, were all the male disciples at this point in the story?

As I read on, I learned that all four canonical gospels identify Mary Magdalene's participation in the central event of Christianity, the Resurrection. All of the gospels identify her as one of the women who went to the tomb three days after the death of Jesus. Only John's gospel says that she went to the tomb alone.

According to John, on the first day of the week while it was still dark, Mary Magdalene went alone to the tomb. Finding it empty and imagining that the body had been stolen by thieves, she ran to tell the disciples. After following her back and confirming for themselves that the tomb was empty, Peter and the others went away, leaving Mary behind.

Overcome with grief, Mary then encountered a man in the garden whom she initially mistook for the gardener. But when Jesus called out her name, she immediately recognized his voice and ran to embrace him.

Jesus held her back, saying, *Noli me tangere. You can't touch me any more.* Every Catholic knows this story.

I knew John's gospel well, having heard it read at Mass every Easter Sunday morning throughout my childhood. It was a beautiful story and just reading it unleashed a flood of fond memories. Pushing my chair back from the computer, I began to pleasantly reflect on the countless Easter Sundays in my past.

I remembered the new clothes, the new hats, the gloves and purses and the fragrance of the carnation corsages that my aunt sent us every year. I remembered the beautiful painted eggs, the chocolate bunnies and yellow marshmallow chicks, and I remembered Easter dinner at my grandmother's house with all of my cousins.

I also remembered the midnight Easter liturgy I had been allowed to attend once I was old enough. This ceremony had included a part that I absolutely loved. At one point in the service, all the lights in the church were turned off, and for several minutes the immense building with its long aisles and huge crucifix suspended above the altar had been in total darkness.

Every parishioner had been given a tiny candle at the entrance to the church, and at the right moment, the priest would come down from the altar into the dark silence and light one person's candle.

Then, one by one, the congregants lit their own candles from each other's until the entire church was ablaze. All the tiny candles glowing in the darkness had been an incredibly beautiful sight.

Looking out the window now, I noticed that dawn had broken. A cover of dew on the grass sparkled in the light of the new day. As I stood up to stretch, the thought of turning off the computer and going back to my warm, cozy bed crossed my mind. But then something stopped me.

Wait a minute, I thought. Wasn't Peter's authority as head of the Church actually based on his having been the first disciple to see Jesus in his resurrected state? Wasn't this fact held up by the Church as the very basis of the doctrine of apostolic succession?

Yet, according to what I had just read Matthew, Mark and John's account had identified Mary Magdalene as the first witness to the Resurrection. Therefore, shouldn't she have been considered the head of the Church?

I immediately sat back down at the computer, determined to find an explanation for this glaring inconsistency. But it wasn't long before I felt myself slipping into a bottomless quagmire of inconsistencies and confusion. In fact, as had been true of my research on the Cathar, the Templar and the royal Merovingians, the deeper I looked into Mary Magdalene's history, the less I understood.

I even found confusion about her name! Did it denote a place of birth, a lineage, or was it a title? The Hebrew translations for *Magdalene* are *tower, watchtower,* or *fortified by towers.*

I remembered that the woman at the night market referred to her as the watchtower. This title reminded me all too well once again of the unaccountable ticking sound I had heard at the strange village of Rennes le Château.

Then, there was the matter of Mary Magdalene's mix-up with other women in the gospel stories. While the Church itself had admitted she was not the woman referred to as the repentant prostitute, many authorities still believed she was actually the woman named Mary of Bethany. This Mary was described in John's gospel as the sister of Martha and Lazarus, and the woman who anointed Jesus' feet with precious spikenard and then dried them with her hair.

As I thought about it, I realized that Father Saunière, the pastor of the ancient village of Rennes Le Château, must certainly have believed Mary Magdalene and Mary of Bethany to be one and the same. His ancient church had been dedicated to Mary Magdalene, he had named his beautiful gothic tower *Magdala*, and he had called his own residence the *Villa Bethania.*

Were Mary Magdalene and Mary of Bethany actually the same woman? If they were why did the Church hide it? And what was the significance of the anointing?

Here things became even more confused. In the ancient Mediterranean world, I learned, kingship had ritually been conferred through an anointing ceremony performed by an heiress or royal priestess acting as a surrogate of the Goddess. In almost every depiction of Mary Magdalene I'd ever seen she had been shown holding an anointing jar in her outstretched hand. Was it possible that Mary Magdalene anointed Jesus king of the Jews? Was it possible that Mary Magdalene was an heiress or royal priestess? And what was this business about the Goddess?

According to what I read, the ancient king-making rite had often included a sacred marriage ceremony between the king and the woman anointing him. Was it possible that this kingship ritual was the reason why Louise had claimed that Mary Magdalene had been married to Jesus? Or was I completely off track now?

As I read on, I learned that once anointed, the king was referred to as the *Messiah* in Hebrew and as the *Christos* in Greek. Jesus certainly had been called by both these names.

This information reminded me of my research of the Merovingians. I clearly remembered reading that the Merovingians had anointed their kings in a public ritual. Had a woman performed the anointing? I also remembered that the Church gave itself the right to appoint kings by taking over this king making ritual after eliminating the Merovingians. I was fairly confident that the Church had continued this ritual anointing in a cathedral in the north of France up until the nineteenth century. Maybe the Church had simply eliminated all parts of the ritual that involved women including the sacred marriage rite.

At this point, overwhelmed with ideas racing through my head, I paused to consider all I had just learned. Maybe, I admitted for the first time, there really was something more to be said for Louise's theory. But how would I ever know?

How would I ever really know if Mary Magdalene had been married to Jesus, if she had come to France, if she had brought with her not just children but a spiritual tradition different from that of the Church? How would I ever know if the entire crusade against the gentle Cathar had intentionally been initiated on her feast day?

Then I had an idea! I needed to talk to Chris and find out what she thought about it. But after looking up at the clock on the wall, I knew it was too early to call her. She and Michael would probably still be asleep. I'd have to wait at least another hour, maybe even two, before phoning her.

What would I do with myself for two hours? Everyone else in the house was still sleeping soundly but I'd never be able to fall back asleep now.

I knew the local *boulangerie* was open, and a walk in the morning sunshine felt like a good idea. Besides, I could pick up a warm *baguette* and some *croissants* for the kids and Bill. Grabbing my sweater from the back of the chair, I headed out the door.

It wasn't until I closed the front gate, however, that I remembered that all of Cugnaux would also be up and out. As I walked into the street, instead of being met by the quiet of a new day, I found myself part of a bustling crowd. It was Saturday, the day of the Cugnaux morning market on the town square. Immediately drawn into the flow of motion, I decided against the *boulangerie* and followed everyone else to town.

The man who sold the bread and *pâtisserie* always set up on the very edge of the square, and I intended to go directly to his stand, pick up what I'd come for and then return home. But I couldn't resist buying a half-dozen delicious-looking peaches from a vegetable and fruit vender along the way. And I couldn't resist petting the two pretty Pyrénées ponies that accompanied the man who sold the lavender honey.

When I finally approached the man with the bread and pastries, he recognized me and called out, "Hello, A-mer-i-can," he said, pronouncing every syllable with care. "How are you today?"

"Very well," I replied, knowing that he enjoyed speaking English, "And how are you?"

"The good Lord has given us a beautiful morning, no?" he replied.

If he only knew what I've been thinking lately about the good Lord, he'd probably never speak to me again, I thought guiltily.

"On this beautiful morning," I said, "I'll have four of your *chocolatines*, four *pain de raisin* and one *baguette*, please."

After paying the *boulanger*, I made one more stop at a flower vendor's stall, where I was drawn to buy a bouquet of the reddest roses I'd ever seen. For Mary Magdalene, I said silently to myself as I handed over the seven *francs* to the merchant, whoever she was.

CHAPTER FIFTEEN

Stories of Mary Magdalene in Stone and Glass

Unless every journey we make brings us face to face with her,
we are going nowhere.

Peter Kingsley, *Reality*

BY THE TIME I RETURNED HOME, the kids and Bill were awake and waiting for me. Rachel met me at the door and took the roses from my hands. "Ouch!" she cried, as she took hold of the flowers, "These are thorny! I'll put them in a vase, OK, Mom?"

"You were up early," said Bill as he came into the kitchen to offer his help. "Want me to make some scrambled eggs?"

When we had finished eating and the breakfast dishes had been washed and put away, the kids settled themselves on the couch to watch TV. Bill went to the desk to look over the week's mail, and after glancing at the clock and assuring myself that Chris and Michael would surely be up by now, I headed to the phone in the bedroom.

"I was hoping it was you," said Chris immediately. "I've been dying to speak with you all morning, but I was afraid I'd be disturbing you if I called. I've barely slept," she continued without pause. "I can't get my mind off what that woman, Louise, told us at the night market. I kept Michael awake all night with my tossing and turning, and now he's off playing in a golf tournament half asleep and in a foul mood. I'm still in my nightgown, buried in books, trying to either confirm or refute what she told us."

"It's the same with me." I replied. "I've been on the computer since before dawn. But I've had an idea. Do you remember Louise telling us that Mary Magdalene had brought both her family and its spiritual tradition with her to the south of France? If that's true," I went on, "don't you think we ought to be able to find some evidence of it in the ancient churches around here?"

"Of course," said Chris excitedly. *The Bible of the Illiterates!* All the stories are told in the stone and glass."

I felt Chris' mounting excitement "If what Louise said is true, we should be able to find lots of verification in the old churches and abbeys around Toulouse. I'll ring Alicia; she'll be so disappointed if we don't ask her to join us. When can we start?"

"I'll be ready to go on Monday," I offered. "I need to get the kids ready for their return to school tomorrow, but after that I'm free."

And so, the following week, as autumn settled in on southern France, Chris, Alicia and I began to explore the Languedoc's Christian legacy. For the next few months, two and sometimes three times weekly, we packed picnic lunches of *baguettes*, cheese and whatever anyone had in their refrigerator that morning, and headed out to investigate the treasures hidden beneath the ribbed and barrel-vaulted canopies of the region's sacred architecture.

Sometimes we started out with a specific destination in mind. Other times we just agreed on a meeting spot and set out to see what we could find. The landscape in and around Toulouse is virtually teeming with religious buildings. Towering church spires rise up imposingly from almost every vista, and even the tiniest of village squares is dominated by an ancient place of prayer. Larger towns boast a cathedral or basilica and scores of monastic sanctuaries lie tucked away in the countryside.

Once we had learned to adjust our eyes to the dim light and haze of the incense smoke, and had accustomed ourselves to the dizzying effects of the architecture, we began to find what we were looking for.

We explored the immense cathedrals in the bustling cities of Narbonne, Bourges and Montpellier and in the smaller towns of Cahors, Bergerac and Auch. We followed the rivers to the ancient monasteries of Moisac, Prouille and to the magically lit Cahors, with its exquisite reliquary of the eleven-year-old martyred girl encrusted with gifts of jewels and gold brought to the saint by pilgrims and kings. And we found our way to the isolated abbeys of Fontfroide, Lagrasse, St-Michel-de-Cuxa, Flauran, and to the hauntingly beautiful solitude of St.Guilhem-le-Désert.

One cold, rainy day, we spent the afternoon in Toulouse. Once the capital of Occitania, Toulouse was the site of several historically important sacred buildings. While it was interesting to learn that one of the forty gold caskets on display in the cathedral of St. Étienne belonged to St. Louis, the canonized French king who died of plague on his return home from the crusades in 1270, this building actually felt a bit creepy and was of little interest to us.

Nor was the city's other great cathedral, Les Jacobins, built by the Dominicans as part of their relentless efforts to impose the will of the Church on the citizens of Toulouse after the crusade against the Cathar. It boasted a macabre gilded reliquary enshrining the head of St. Thomas Aquinas.

The basilica of St. Sernin is without question the most outstanding religious building in Toulouse. Before the Romans, the place where the beautiful basilica now stands was a Celtic site of worship, and the altar table survives from that time.

"It's a perfect example," said Alicia, "of how the Christians simply hijacked the sites that had been sacred for centuries."

It was, however, the very dark and damp basilica of Notre-Dame-de-la-Daurade that took our attention. Built like St. Sernin on the site of an ancient Roman temple, Notre-Dame-de-la-Daurade, along the Garonne River, was difficult to find, its entrance hardly distinguishable from the buildings that surround it. While the basilica was obviously of little importance to other tourists, it was of great interest to us.

On a poorly lit altar, barely visible through the darkness, clothed in an elaborate gown was displayed a completely black Madonna and child. I had never seen anything like her before. She was absolutely beautiful and a palpable air of mystery surrounded her.

"It's a Black Virgin," whispered Chris, pointing to the statue through the darkness.

"Why is it black?" I whispered in response. A few old women saying the rosary in the front pew cast an annoyed look at us, and Chris pointed to the door. Alicia followed along behind.

"The Church," Chris said, when we were once again outside, "attributed the blackness of the virgin and her child to either soot from the candle smoke or exposure to the elements. They claim the Black Madonnas, which are found all over Europe but mostly in France, were not originally intended to be black, but only became so by accident."

"But most authorities dismiss that explanation as total rubbish," interrupted Alicia, coming up behind us. "They are black by design. All of the Black Virgins are pre-Christian or are copies of older versions. So the Church has a difficult time explaining their existence at all."

"Pre-Christian?" I asked. "You mean the black statue isn't the Virgin Mary? That's not baby Jesus on her lap?"

"No," replied Alicia emphatically. "The Black Virgin has nothing to do with Jesus or his mother Mary, despite the striking resemblance the statue has to the Madonna and child that's familiar to every Christian."

"Well, then, who is she?" I asked, fascinated.

"I don't think anyone knows for sure," said Alicia. "I've heard she is the ancient Goddess of the Egyptians, Isis. Maybe she is Sophia, the Greek Goddess of wisdom.

"I do know for certain that many of the ancient Black Virgin sites were lavishly restored during the time of the Merovingians, and that St. Bernard had a great interest in the statues. There was a Black Virgin in the town where he was born and supposedly he received three drops of milk from another when he was a baby."

"Bernard was nursed by a Black Madonna?" I asked sarcastically.

"I've heard," said Chris, "that she also might be the *Dark Bride* described in the ancient Hebrew *Song of Songs*."

"I know for certain," replied Alicia, that Bernard was obsessed with the Song of Songs. He gave hundreds of sermons on the topic. I think the poem was originally written as an accompaniment to the ancient king anointing rituals."

"Then that would connect the Black Virgins to Mary Magdalene." I added.

Chris and Alicia both turned to me with a surprised look.

"In the gospel of John, Mary Magdalene anointed Jesus as king, didn't she?" I asked.

"That's very interesting," said Alicia. "I've never considered Mary Magdalene might be connected to the Black Madonnas. I'm certain though that the Song of Songs is read as part of the liturgy on her feast day. That can't possibly be a coincidence."

"If she was connected to the anointing ritual," said Chris. "That would explain why she is so often shown holding a jar of oil in her hand."

"Yes," concluded Alicia, "it might also explain a lot more as well."

During our explorations of the religious buildings, we encountered Mary Magdalene in one form or another in almost every church, monastery and cathedral we visited. The prevalence of these images confirmed to us without question that she had been one of the most beloved saints in medieval France.

We had seen the Magdalene depicted in her scarlet cloak at the foot of the crucifix when all the male disciples had been frightened away. We had seen her in the first light of dawn on her way to the tomb, and we had seen her outside the empty sepulcher on Easter morning as the first witness to the Resurrection.

In addition to these familiar images, we had often come across a curious depiction of her standing at the bow of a small boat with her outstretched hand holding her alabaster jar. But never in our travels had we found an explanation for this peculiar scene.

Then one day, while visiting the bookstore in the cathedral of Bourges, Alicia held up a book, and called out to us across the store, "I've found it!" she said.

"Found what?" asked Chris as the two of us came up next to her.

"It's the *Golden Legend*, the 12th century *official* life stories of the saints," explained Alicia. "It's what we've been looking for! It has the story of Mary Magdalene's life in France!"

We purchased the book, hurried out to a bench in front of the cathedral and turned to the section on Mary Magdalene.

According to the author, a Dominican monk, exactly fourteen years after the crucifixion, Mary Magdalene, Lazarus, her brother, whom Jesus had raised from the dead, and a small entourage, was sent out into the Mediterranean Sea on a tiny boat without rudder or pilot. Miraculously, the tiny boat washed up at the port of Marseilles, France, with all on board safe and sound.

After the boat landing, Mary Magdalene disembarked and immediately began preaching the word of Jesus *more profusely than any other* and performing amazing miracles, including bringing a dead knight back to life. In old age she had retreated to a contemplative life in the wilderness and when she died, had been buried near Aix-en-Provence where her relics were worshiped until they were moved to Burgundy to protect them from Saracen invasion.

"Well," Chris said conclusively, "That means at the very least someone else besides our friend, Louise, at the night market believes Mary Magdalene actually lived in France."

"So," Alicia concluded, "all we need to do now is to find some evidence that Mary Magdalene and Jesus were husband and wife and all the rest of the pieces of the puzzle will fit neatly in place."

I wasn't so sure how neatly it would all fit together. There was still the matter of the "other" spiritual tradition to be dealt with. And if there really was an "other" tradition, did it involve the Cathar?

A few days later, Anne, who had introduced Chris to me at the Americans in Toulouse tea, asked if she could join us on a trip we were planning to a nearby monastery at Flauran. Anne did not usually travel with us and was unfamiliar with the direction our investigations had recently taken. Without giving it a second thought, however, we welcomed her along.

The gardens of the monastery at Flauran were as beautiful as any we had seen. As we sat relaxing in the warm autumn sun, listening to the gentle splashing of the cloister fountain Alicia suddenly broke in.

"Guess what! I've been researching St. James lately, and I'm convinced that he was actually Jesus' brother."

"What?" exclaimed Anne, jumping up from where she had been sitting. "Jesus didn't have any brothers! His mother was a virgin, remember? It's irrefutable Church doctrine."

"Come on, Anne," said Alicia, "The virginity of Mary is a myth. Her virginity was never intended to be taken literally. I'm certain Jesus had brothers and probably sisters, too."

"That is the most ridiculous thing I've ever heard you say," said Anne, looking around at Chris and me for confirmation. "I can't believe you're serious."

I knew exactly what Anne was feeling. She had grown up Catholic, as had I, and her conditioning now prohibited her from thinking such thoughts.

"Alicia, you don't know any of that for sure," I cautioned.

"I'll wager that Jesus had a wife and children as well," continued Alicia. "Remember, he was a Jew of royal descent. The Old Testament emphasizes that bloodlines meant everything. Of course he was married, of course he had children. He was heir to the Line of David, and all heirs have children—they have to."

Anne glared at Alicia and just shook her head.

"Hey, why don't we go take a look at the monastery's church," suggested Chris, anxious to end the discussion.

Anne was still seething as we got up and walked across the monastery's garden toward the Church. When we were met at the door by an elderly monk who offered his services as a tour guide, she seemed to calm down. As we made our way through the ancient building, the gentle monk pointed out the features of historic and architectural significance.

But just when it seemed Anne had finally forgotten our previous discussion, Alicia blurted out a question to the monk. "By the way," she asked "did Jesus have any brothers?"

The words landed on our white-mantled tour guide as if they had been shot from a gun. He gasped, his large eyes grew wide, and his mouth actually fell open. "You want to know if Jesus had brothers? Have I heard you correctly?" he asked Alicia, his voice rising in disbelief.

She slowly nodded her head, looking as if she regretted having asked what she now realized to be an inflammatory question.

With exaggerated movements, the monk swung his body around to face Chris. "Is she... one of the... infidels? Is she a heretic?" he asked.

Then, without waiting for an answer, he spun back around toward Alicia and, to our amazement, lifted his hand in the air as if threatening to strike her.

"No! No! No!" he cried, as we watched in stunned silence. "There was only one Virgin Birth! Only one!"

But he didn't stop there. He continued, his face reddening, "None of the other children born to Mary was immaculately conceived!"

What? What had he just said? Had he just actually confirmed that Jesus did have siblings? I turned around to look at Anne, who was behind me, and saw the entire gamut of emotions I had experienced these past months now cross her face.

She touched my hand and then whispered to me, "Other children? What... other... children? Is he saying that there were other children?"

The monk, now eager to change the subject and seemingly embarrassed by his outburst, grabbed Chris' hand and gently pulled her along through the stone gallery, Alicia and I trailing silently after them.

Thankfully, our tour soon came to an end, and once outside again in the sunlight, we walked directly to the car.

Anne was the first to speak. "Well," she said, "if Jesus had a brother, then why not a sister? And if he had a sister, then why not a wife? Why not kids?" Then, looking up at us, she admitted sadly, "I've been such a fool."

Back in the car, we rode along silently, each of us deep in our own thoughts. Finally, Alicia broke the silence. "The church fathers despised women and sex, it's that simple. Jesus had to have had a mother but the Church couldn't let him or her get mixed up with a dirty little thing like sex. Thomas Aquinas, the 13th century Christian philosopher, said that God had made a *mistake* when He created women. A bloody *mistake!* Can you believe that? Now what kind of God makes a *mistake?* Did you know that a council of bishops in the sixth century actually voted on whether or not women had souls? The Church didn't just ban books at the Council of Nicea—it banned women!"

"Alicia..." Anne started in protest but then abruptly stopped.

"They virtually wiped the ancient tradition of the Goddess from the face of the Earth," continued Alicia.

"It's a hard pill to swallow, no matter how you look at it," said Chris.

"You mean, accepting that Mary wasn't a virgin and that Jesus had a wife and children?" asked Alicia. "I don't understand why you guys are struggling so hard with all of this,"

"That's because you weren't brought up Catholic," said Anne. "You didn't have these concepts drummed into your head daily by every adult in your world. You don't feel betrayed by people you trusted as spiritual authorities."

"I don't think it was just the Catholics who were taught this stuff," said Chris. "I think the majority of the Christian world has always believed most of the traditional Jesus story. How many people do you know who would write you off their invite list once they learned you seriously believed Mary Magdalene, the repentant whore, had been the wife of Jesus and the mother of his children?"

"Hey, wait a minute!" interrupted Anne, "Doesn't the gospel of Matthew open with a genealogy of Joseph, the husband of Mary? Doesn't it begin with Abraham and continue through David, with lots of *begettings* in between?"

"Right," said Chris, "The vicar reads Matthew's birth narrative at my Church every Christmas morning."

"Isn't the purpose of this passage to show that Jesus was a descendent of the royal Davidic line through his father?" asked Anne.

I started to laugh when I realized her point.

"What? What's so funny?" asked Chris, coloring slightly.

"If Mary was a virgin, what would be the point of showing Joseph's lineage?" asked Anne.

"Exactly," said Alicia. "No sperm, no bloodline. Don't you see how amazingly illogical it all is?"

CHAPTER SIXTEEN

The Outlawed Books

> And at the same time she wants everything that
> you think you already have: your cleverness, your imagined ability
> to decide and argue and choose. She wants you.
> She absolutely insists that you follow her, wherever she will lead.
>
> Peter Kingsley, *Reality*

SOON AFTER OUR ENCOUNTER with the monk and his revelation about Jesus' family, Alicia, Chris, and I decided to take a break, at least temporarily, from investigating the religious buildings. The winter holidays were approaching and each of us had family responsibilities requiring our attention. We agreed to continue with our research independently, promising to call one another if we happened upon anything earth-shattering.

It hadn't even been a week since our decision to take a break when, late one night on the computer, I stumbled across the fascinating history of an ancient Egyptian library. According to what I read, the library had been established in about 300 B.C.E. in the port city of Alexandria and had served as a haven for philosophers, scientists, musicians and mystics, all of whom came to Alexandria seeking inspiration.

It was at this very library, I learned, that Eratosthenes had measured the diameter of the Earth, Euclid had discovered the laws of geometry, and Herophilus had established the rules of anatomy and physiology. In fact, I learned, the entire scholarship of the ancient world had at one time been housed in this library.

Then, in the fourth century, the ancient building and all that it held had been burned to the ground by an angry mob of Christian monks. It made me sick to my stomach to imagine all that had been lost. An estimated 300,000 to 700,000 scrolls and manuscripts had gone up in flames, including original works of Plato, Socrates and Pythagoras.

Lost as well, I learned, had been the literature of the *ancient mystery traditions* and texts attributed to early Christian groups called Gnostics.

Coming across the word, Gnostics, stopped me. I had seen the term used before in regard to the Cathar, but I had never really understood its meaning. Now, I decided to quickly check the definition and get right back to what I was reading about the library of Alexandria.

I learned that Gnostic, which derives from the Greek word *gnosis,* meaning *to know from direct experience,* is a collective term given to a variety of ancient mystical teachings. The Gnostic teachings emphasize salvation through personal revelation and a direct knowledge of truth. According to what I read, the Gnostics, who claimed to possess the true, secret teachings of Jesus, were denounced as heretics and enemies of the Church at the Council of Nicea. From that day on, they were violently suppressed, their scriptures burned and all memories of them erased from history.

The Gnostics' claim that they possessed the true teachings of Jesus reminded me of the Cathar. Both groups emphasized a direct experience of truth. The Cathar found theirs within the sacrament they called the *consolamentum.*

As I continued to read about the early Christian Gnostics, all but forgetting the library of Alexandria, I learned that in 1945 in Upper Egypt, an Arab peasant had amazingly stumbled upon a large earthenware jar and discovered inside thirteen papyrus books bound in leather. The collection of books, believed to have been hidden away by Christian monks from a nearby monastery sixteen hundred years earlier, were revealed to be primarily the writings of the early Christians Gnostics.

Now known as the *Nag Hammadi Library,* named after the town where the books had been found, the texts are believed by scholars to be at least as old as the Orthodox gospels themselves. Included among the preserved Gnostic texts were also a fragmented copy of Plato's *Republic,* a text that claims Zoroastrian heritage, another, in a particularly poor state of preservation, called simply, *Melchizedek,* and a hermetic text that presents mystical dialogues of *initiation* between someone named Hermes Trismegistus and his son, Tat. I was fascinated.

As I read on, I learned that among these early Christian writings, some of which had been specifically outlawed as early as the second century, were intriguing titles such as *The Secret Gospel of Mark, The Gospel of Thomas, The Secret Book of John, The Secret Book of James, The Gospel of Truth,* and *The Gospel of the Egyptians.*

When I began to read the actual translated texts, I found that many introduced themselves as *the secret and hidden teachings of Jesus.* My head tingled as I read the opening to the *Apocryphon of John* as it offered to *reveal the mysteries and the things hidden in silence.*

The Gospel of Thomas began with: "These are the secret sayings which the living Jesus spoke… and whoever finds the interpretation of these sayings will not experience death."

Many of the texts were amazingly complex and difficult to understand, using words I'd never before heard. But others I found to be poetic and very beautiful. The text entitled, *The Gospel of Truth,* was particularly beautiful. "The gospel of truth," it begins, "is joy."

This text speaks in images of fragrant perfumes, dense fog, and the light of dawn. It describes the spirit as chasing the self, Christ as *the light with no shadow,* and the Father as the *physician, who goes to the place where sickness dwells.* The language of *The Gospel of Truth* is light, and its glowing imagery had a powerful effect on me.

As I read, I felt myself slowly being lifted above the cynicism, sense of betrayal, and anger that I'd recently felt towards the Church. *The Gospel of Truth* spoke in a language that, in some magical way, my soul understood, and was as soothing as a lullaby.

Then, I sat up with a start. According to *The Gospel of Truth, those whom he has anointed are the ones that have become perfect.*

The words, *anointed* and *perfect* stopped me cold. It was as if every cell in my body was awake and alert. *Perfect* was the name given to the Cathar who had taken the only Cathar sacrament, the *consolamentum.*

In French, the initiates had been called, *Parfait.* The authors of my Cathar books had often cited the word, *perfect,* as a way to denigrate the Cathar. But now here was this term, *perfect,* being used to denote *those whom he has anointed.* Could the usage of this word simply be a coincidence?

Speculations I had previously read on the derivation of the word had always left the Cathar looking foolish. But the specific use of the word in *The Gospel of Truth* made the hair on the back of my arms stand up. I sensed I was closer to understanding the medieval people who had made their homes in the castles of Peyrepertuse, Puivert and Montségur, and the people who had made their home in my heart since I had first learned of them, than I had ever been.

I held my breath as I considered that these outlawed books of Nag Hammadi, these sacred Gnostic texts hidden away by monks more than 1,600 years ago in the dry desert sands of Egypt, these ancient books that had miraculously survived centuries of book burnings, might actually bring me to an understanding of the Cathar. My pulse began to race as I read on into the night.

I found many references in the *Gnostic Gospels of Nag Hammadi* to Mary Magdalene, and nowhere was she described as a sexual sinner, a prostitute or a repentant whore. In fact, her role in these forbidden texts strongly contrasted with the images of her that I remembered from my childhood.

Here she was spoken of as *the woman who knew the All, the Inheritor of the Light, the Messenger of the esoteric revelation, the chief disciple, and the herald of the new Life.*

In the *Gospels of Nag Hammadi,* Mary Magdalene matched the description of the Mary Magdalene described by Louise at the night market. These ancient, outlawed texts confirmed that Mary Magdalene undeniably held a leadership position in the early Christian community.

But nothing I read, claimed that she had been the wife of Jesus. There wasn't a word that tempted me to believe that Mary Magdalene had been more than an important member of Jesus' entourage and the central witness to the Resurrection.

That is, until I read *The Gospel of Phillip.*

Bound into the same volume with *The Gospel of Thomas, The Gospel of Phillip* was the Gnostic Gospel that completely took my breath away. It was the book we had been looking for, the book neither Chris, Alicia nor I had ever seriously expected to find.

In it, the Greek word, *koinonos,* is used to describe the relationship between Mary Magdalene and Jesus, a word, I learned, that clearly indicates a sexual relationship. According to *The Gospel of Phillip,* Jesus loved Mary Magdalene more than any of the other disciples, and *used to kiss her often on the mouth,* offending the rest of the disciples.

"Why do you love her more than all of us?" the disciples ask Jesus in this gospel, to which Jesus answers, "Why do I not love you as I love her?"

I was stunned. While it seemed that I should no longer be surprised or disturbed by my discoveries of Church deceptions and the lengths to which it had gone to hide what threatened its own power, each time I'd had to face this reality, I'd been astounded.

While I wanted to read more of the *Gnostic Gospels,* I found myself unable to focus. I pushed the chair back from my computer desk, shaking with anger. The full realization that the Church had concealed the true relationship between Mary Magdalene and Jesus was almost too much for me to handle. How would I ever integrate it all?

The Church had burned down a library that contained the entire scholarship of the ancient world.

The Church had attempted and almost succeeded to reduce to ashes any interpretation of Jesus' teachings that promoted a path to inner spiritual knowledge.

The Church had brutally executed millions of people for their refusal to be controlled.

The Church had maligned Saint Mary Magdalene, and then gone on to malign and subjugate every woman.

The Church had decried natural, loving sexuality and made sinful the bond between a man and a woman.

Looking up at the clock, I was surprised to see the lateness of the hour. Everyone else had gone to sleep long ago. When I turned off the computer and stood up, I nearly collapsed from exhaustion, both physical and emotional. As I picked up my empty teacup and blew out the candle I'd been burning, I also noted how cold and dark the house had become.

Almost as soon as I had put my head down on the pillow, I was asleep. In no time at all, however, my sleep was disturbed by the girl from Montségur. As always in my dreams, she was calling to me, asking me to follow her. But where was she taking me? Where would this all end?

In the days that followed my discovery of the outlawed gospels, signs of the coming holidays began popping up everywhere. Every little village and town seemed to have its own special seasonal decorations. Strung across the main streets were festive white lights spelling out holiday messages such as *Joyeuse Saison, Bon Nöel,* or *Bonne Année.*

In addition to the lights, each little village and town also set up a Christmas *crèche* in front of the local church. Though some were small and some quite large, every *crèche* displayed the same familiar statues of Mary and Joseph, the shepherds and kings, the donkeys and lambs and baby Jesus in the manger.

The *crèche* had always played a central role in the traditions of Christmas for me. As a child I'd looked forward to the day it was set up in our parish church. I remembered the smell of the fresh straw in the manger and of the pine boughs amongst the statues as if it were yesterday. I remembered the star that shone from the roof of the stable and all the bright red poinsettias and tall white candles that surrounded it. To me, the *crèche* had always represented good things; family, tradition, promise, hope, peace and joy.

But this year I felt very, very different.

This year it was impossible for me to ignore the fact that the little babe in the manger surrounded by the gentle donkeys and lambs, adored by his beautiful mother and handsome father, awed by the young shepherd boys, and honored by the three wise kings, had grown up to be identified as the founder of the same institution that had ordered the horrific fire at Montségur.

The holiday just didn't feel the same to me anymore. Looking at the *crèche* this year, all I could think of was the complete decimation of medieval Occitania, the annihilation of the Merovingian dynasty, the burning of the great library of antiquity at Alexandria, and the savage Inquisition, which had prided itself on having *roasted to death over a slow fire* the last known grand master of the Templar Knights, Jacques de Molay.

How could I possibly forget that the very same institution associated with Jesus in the manger had systematically maligned all women and successfully vilified Saint Mary Magdalene and the teachings she had brought to France?

The statues seemed almost sinister to me now, and the traditions themselves corrupt. But despite my own feelings, I did not want my family to lose all the magic and excitement of Christmas. So, while we hadn't brought any of our Christmas decorations from the States, I was determined to make a beautiful holiday for my husband and children.

During the month of December, Rachel, Nicholas, Bill and I spent our time together making new decorations with which to celebrate our first Christmas in France. We sewed Christmas stockings of wool and felt, and embellished them with lace, sequins, and golden braid. We made a lovely wreath for our front door with greenery from the yard and adorned it with a handsome burgundy colored satin ribbon. And we bought a little *sapin de Nöel* (the French do not have tall Christmas trees like the ones we had at home), and trimmed it with popcorn, cranberries and a few very special Christmas balls we bought from *Nouvelle Galleries* in downtown Toulouse.

At every free moment, I continued to peruse the Christian *Gnostic Gospels of Nag Hammadi*. Every reading reinforced my decision not to include a *crèche* in our Christmas decorations.

Shopping for groceries during the holidays was a family event in which everyone wanted to participate. The local markets and groceries stores were overflowing with festive fare.

The primary way the French celebrate Christmas is by preparing food, and I had no problem at all participating fully in this way.

The Saturday morning market in our village of Cugnaux was a gourmand's delight. On display was an enormous variety of things to eat, some ready for immediate cooking, some still walking around, very much alive. There were live chickens, turkeys, pheasants, long-necked geese and other fowl. There were also live rabbits, lambs and small wild pigs.

The mushroom selection at the Cugnaux market was also amazing, featuring huge mushrooms that could easily be featured in fairy stories–the kind that had gnomes, elves, and other small creatures of the forest sleeping under them. These mushrooms are called *cepes*, and are beloved by the French of the Languedoc.

In addition to the Cugnaux market, the large grocery stores such as *Carrefour* were also a treat during the holidays. While always very crowded, the selection was worth the bother.

Specialty foods such as *foie gras*, caviar, fancy olives, Toulousian *cassoulet* and *escargot* were available at *Carrefour*, all specially prepared and elegantly packaged for Christmas. And then there were the *pâtisseries*. There were *tartes* and *gateaux*, custards, flans, *crèmes* and *meringues*. There were beautiful Yule log cakes called *Buche de Nöel*, cookies of all varieties, and King Cakes each of which included a crown in the package and a prize hidden inside the cake itself.

In preparation for Christmas, besides making decorations and shopping for food, I decided it was time for a major tidying up of the computer desk. It was covered with stacks of articles I had printed off the Internet, books, note cards and piles of brochures I'd picked up during our tours of the religious buildings.

One afternoon, while organizing the brochures from the monasteries we had visited I became distracted and began reminiscing about our experiences in these buildings. During our travels, all of us had developed a particular fondness for the quiet and seclusion of the abbeys and monasteries of the region. We found these monastic sanctuaries, while no longer occupied by the monks and nuns, to have somehow maintained a penetrating, pervasive and totally seductive spiritual vitality.

The gentle splashing of water from the cloister fountains, the pungent smells of the herb gardens, and the hypnotic tolling of the bells marking the liturgical rhythms of matins and vespers seemed to define a spirituality unrelated to any church or sect.

Our guidebooks often described these buildings as primitive and austere. While it was true that they contained almost none of the religious iconography and decoration we were seeking, we loved these communities and frequently lost hours there just sitting silently beneath the arched galleries of their cloisters or within the timeless calm and coolness of their gardens.

In our travels we had visited monasteries built by the Benedictines, Dominicans, Franciscans, Jesuits and others. But as I looked through the brochures I'd collected, something interesting occurred to me. Though none of us seemed to have noticed it previously, as I thought about it now, the medieval monasteries we had liked the best, the ones in which we had spent the most time and the ones in which we had each felt connected to something greater than ourselves, all had been built by the same monastic order, St. Bernard's Cistercians, the white-robed monastic arm of the Templar Knights. Was this just a… But I stopped myself from even thinking the word, "coincidence."

I quickly phoned Chris with my discovery.

"What do you think it means?" she asked.

"It seems significant," I replied, "but I don't know how."

"Interestingly enough," Chris continued, "I happened upon some information regarding St. Bernard, myself. I had planned to call you today to tell you about it. I discovered that St. Bernard used the bee as his personal seal. What do you make of that? Another coincidence?"

I immediately remembered the illuminated bees in my strange dream of the Merovingian king. The bees had absorbed the king's light and then flown off with it into the night. I didn't know what to make of what Chris had just told me. But hearing that St. Bernard had used the bee as his seal, as had the ancient royal Merovingians, gave me the sensation of sliding another long sought-after puzzle piece right into place.

Throughout the week between Christmas and New Year's, I hardly had a moment to myself. Finally, one chilly night, when Bill had gone for a walk with the kids, I had a moment to look up the Cistercians on the computer. I learned that under the direction of St. Bernard, the Cistercians had been the principal disseminators of a revolutionary style of architecture later defined as Gothic. I also discovered that one of the most important Gothic cathedrals ever built contained an ancient Black Virgin. It was the famous cathedral at Chartres in the north of France, not far from Paris.

Then, on New Year's Eve, after the kids had gone to bed, I decided to try out a new CD that I'd received as a Christmas gift from a dear friend in the States. After quickly glancing at the cover, I decided that the music would not disturb Bill, who was nodding off on the couch beside me. It might even have a comforting effect.

To my complete surprise, however, as the music began to play, our living room was flooded with unexpectedly passionate and haunting melodies and rhythms. They split the previously sleepy ambiance into fragments of color and form, and carried us far away from our warm living room into what I can only describe as a stimulating, yet soothing medieval world of ancient archetypal memories.

Fountains of crimson, deep forest green and amber light spilled into the room and seemed to explode in all directions. Whirling, joyous voices leaped on the air and conjured images of trade fairs, and *troubadours*, of herbal elixirs and illuminated manuscripts.

And then, suddenly, the music twisted and turned and plunged us with tremendous energy into a dark cavern of sacred poetry and psalms where images of darkly clad nuns soulfully swayed beneath ribbed vaulted ceilings.

After several minutes of being completely turned upside down and transfixed by the sounds, I reached for the liner notes and discovered that we were listening to a composition recorded in a Gothic cathedral of a twelfth century German Christian mystic named Hildegard von Bingin.

The liner notes included a short biography of Hildegard's life. As I read out loud to Bill, who was now wide awake and equally enthralled by the music, we learned that Hildegard had been born in 1098, and at the age of eight had been given as a tithe by her parents to an abbey.

Evidently, Hildegard had, even as a child, been inclined to visions. Her ecstatic experiences had increased in intensity as she matured, and she began describing them in poetry and music.

After Hildegard's death, three nuns from her order had reported seeing her moving radiantly through the cloister late at night chanting one of her finest creative efforts, "Praise to the Mother." In fact, most of her compositions, I read, had been dedicated to the *Divine Mother*.

I was amazed when I read further on and discovered that Hildegard's mentor had been none other than the enigmatic St. Bernard himself!

There was no need, I concluded, to keep questioning these coincidences—they were clearly no such thing. I didn't know what it all meant, but after hearing Hildegard's amazing music, I did know with absolute certainty that I had to go see the Black Virgin in Bernard's gothic masterpiece in the north of France, the cathedral of Chartres.

CHAPTER SEVENTEEN

The Journey North:
Chambord and Leonardo

> Traveling along the path pointed out by the Goddess
> is a matter of tremendous speed. She has already moved off,
> and there is not a moment to wait or think. You are either
> with her or you are not. Either you follow the signs
> on the path—or you will be left behind,
> again with the ghosts at the fork in the road.
>
> Peter Kingsley, *Reality*

THE NEXT DAY, I telephoned Chris, Alicia and Anne and asked them if they would like to go with me to Chartres. Anne's previously arranged trip to Turkey kept her from joining us, but Chris enthusiastically agreed. "I've wanted to see the cathedral in Chartres since I was a child," she said.

Alicia simply asked, "When do we leave?"

Our subsequent travel arrangements fell easily into place, and three days later we were off on an eight-hundred kilometer trip north, by far the longest trip we'd ever made together.

We departed Toulouse in the crispness of the early morning, and by mid-afternoon the rugged, untamed countryside of the Languedoc had given way to the well-mannered plains, tidy cultivated fields and sophisticated French provincial architecture of the North.

On what seemed a whim, we decided to make a short stop in the Loire River Valley, world famous for its beautiful royal châteaux. We approached the region in the late afternoon, and as we curved along the river's edge, the landscape slowly opened up into what felt like a playground of lush gardens and tamed forests. Signs along the road pointed the way to each of the architectural achievements that, during the fifteenth and sixteenth century, had been the luxurious country homes of the French royal families and aristocracy.

As we drove along, Chris read the descriptions of the countless châteaux from our guidebook. We agreed that we had time to visit just one of them if we were to make it to Chartres by nightfall. From amongst the hundreds of possibilities, we selected the Château Chambord which, from what we read, had been the favorite home of the French king, François 1st.

In retrospect, none of us was quite sure why we'd selected this particular château or even what criteria had assisted us in making our choice. Nevertheless, while our guidebook had described Chenonceau as the most romantic, Cheverny as the most elegant, Loches as the most interesting, and Amboise as the finest royal residence on the Loire, the three of us agreed unanimously on Chambord as our stopping point.

We followed the signs and soon turned off the main road. After traversing a long and narrow tree-lined drive, we arrived in front of the grand Chambord. Our first impression of the enormous château was of an incredibly asymmetrical confusion of turrets, towers, dormers, chimneys and gables.

Its sheer size was awesome but as we made our way to its entrance, a single feature froze us in our tracks. Sculpted into the stone, on the main cylindrical towers, were two enormous salamanders.

The sight literally took my breath away and my knees became weak. "Oh, my gosh!" I exclaimed, remembering all too well my strange encounter with the salamanders at the foot of Montségur, and then again at Rennes le Château.

Chris and Alicia, familiar with my relationship with salamanders, stood silent for several seconds, staring in bewilderment at the emblems on the towers. "Can this possibly be just another coincidence?" Chris finally asked.

"I've given up using that word," I said. "As far as I'm concerned, we're being guided along some invisible path. I don't know how else to describe it, but I think I finally accept it."

"It's like the fairy story, Hansel and Gretel, said Chris. "Only in the fairy story, the children followed pebbles home. We're following bees and salamanders."

"And Black Virgins," added Alicia.

We were soon to learn that the salamanders had been the royal seal of François 1st, and according to the book we purchased at the château's gift shop, no fewer than seven hundred of them graced his home at Chambord.

Under the sign of the salamanders, we learned that François had built, with the aid of his court architect, Leonardo da Vinci, the Loire Valley's largest château, boasting over four hundred rooms and surrounded by a 13,000 acre reserve.

"Leonardo da Vinci was the court architect of a French king? This is certainly news to me!" breathed Chris, impressed beyond words.

We also learned from the château guidebook that the thirty-two-year reign of François the First, beginning in 1515, is often regarded as the most creative in French history.

François' greatest achievements centered around his importing of the philosophy, art and literature of Renaissance Italy to France. After having been educated in Florence, François had become the admirer and friend of many of the great Renaissance artists, particularly Leonardo da Vinci.

As we walked through the seemingly endless maze of rooms—a vaulted ballroom, an elegant chapel, a gallery of royal portraits, and François' bedroom with its luxuriously embroidered red velvet bed curtains—we eventually found ourselves directly in front of Chambord's most renowned feature, a white marble double staircase.

The staircase was truly an amazing sight. It consisted of two separate flights of stairs, each one circling around the other in a symmetry that was totally mind-boggling and yet incredibly graceful. The staircase was described in our guidebook as a double helix in stone, built wide enough for use by both people and horses. As Alicia and Chris walked around marveling at the fantastic design, I let myself wander into a room off the main hall.

The large room featured walls decorated in richly woven tapestries illustrating the hunt, but the focal point was a white marble fireplace the size of one of the walls. A fire in the massive fireplace blazed and crackled loudly.

As I walked through the room, I noticed immediately that the air, while clouded in smoke, felt charged with an unusual energy. I moved close to the heat of the fire to warm my hands and as I felt the warmth from the flames relax my body, a sensation I hadn't felt in a long time came over me.

The next thing I knew, the room, which only seconds before had been totally empty, came alive. Robust voices and the sounds of laughter and merriment rang through the air. Richly attired lords and ladies filled the hall. They wore coats of shiny, dark leather, deep-colored velvet with pearl and gemstone buttons, and exquisitely embroidered linen with collars and sleeves of fur.

Their feathered hats, leather gloves and boots, and rosy cheeks suggested that they'd just returned from a long day's hunt in the January chill. The smell of chestnuts roasting in the fire, the pungent scent of horses and saddle leather mingled with the aromas of meat cooking somewhere close by.

A man, whom I recognized immediately as King François from his portraits hanging throughout the château, was the center of attention. He laughed loudly and waved his arms as he spoke. Three sleek-looking hunting dogs lay attentively at his feet as the guests raised their crystal goblets to toast him.

In the back of the room, far away from the fire, I caught sight of a bearded man who stood out from all the others. He seemed to be watching, rather than participating in the festivities. As I looked at him more closely, I saw that embroidered on his scarlet hat was a golden bee.

When his deeply creased eyes met mine, a smile of recognition formed on his face and he immediately began walking toward me.

And then I felt a hand on my shoulder.

"I'm freezing," said Chris. "Are you ready to go?"

Suddenly the room fell silent. Although I was completely disoriented, not sure where I was, or even what century I was in, I automatically nodded my head in response.

As we walked away from the blazing fire, I struggled to find the words to explain to Chris what I'd just experienced, despite my awareness that there were no words to relate what had occurred.

"I'm so sorry," said Chris, after I'd described my experience as best I could. "If I'd known what was going on, I never would have interrupted."

"It's all right," I said. "I was a little frightened anyway. I'm not comfortable losing control over myself like that. I never know what's going to happen."

"I think it sounds fascinating," said Chris. "I wish I could have such amazing experiences."

"That staircase," Alicia excitedly called out as she came running up behind us. "It's just fantastic, isn't it?"

Chris and I both agreed, and also agreed that we'd better get going. It was late afternoon by the time we were back in the car, and after a quick glance at the map, we realized that we'd have to hurry if we were going to make Chartres before dark.

Alicia agreed to drive, and I crawled into the back seat hoping for a little nap and some time to consider what I had just experienced. It had seemed as if the man in the scarlet hat was going to speak to me. What, I wondered, was he about to say?

"It says here in the guidebook," said Chris, once we were back on the highway, "that Leonardo da Vinci lived at Chambord for several years and might have actually designed that amazing marble staircase. I'd no idea that Leonardo ever lived in France. But now that I think about it, I've wondered how the Mona Lisa came to be at the Louvre rather than at the Uffizi in Florence."

"François offered sanctuary in France to his friend, Leonardo da Vinci," Alicia informed us, "after he'd fallen out of favor with the Church and feared for his life in Florence. He bequeathed the Mona Lisa and many other of his most cherished paintings to the royal French coffers, and died in the arms of François."

"Alicia," said Chris, "Your breadth of knowledge never fails to amaze me. But what could Leonardo possibly have done to set himself at odds with the Church? The themes of so many of his paintings are deeply religious and definitely orthodox, aren't they?"

"There are actually some questions about how orthodox Leonardo's religious paintings really are," replied Alicia. "His patron, Còsimo de Mèdici, the grandfather of Lorenzo the Magnificent and patron to Botticelli and Michelangelo, definitely had a difficult relationship with the Church. At least some of Còsimo's problems with the authorities in Rome were related to his library of ancient manuscripts and the philosophy they extolled."

"What exactly was in his library?" I asked, suddenly revived by the fascinating turn of our conversation.

"Well," replied Alicia, "apparently some of the books Còsimo owned and others he was hoping to purchase had actually been outlawed by the Church centuries earlier. Còsimo evidently had agents throughout the world searching for ancient manuscripts to bring back to Florence. Once he had them in his possession, Marsilio Ficino, a Florentine monk, translated the texts for him. I've read that many of the texts in the Mèdici collection were survivors of the great fire at the Alexandria library."

"There were books saved from the fire at the Alexandria library?" I asked, having completely given up my idea of a nap.

"Evidently so," said Alicia. "In fact, when Còsimo was quite old and near death, he had made an important purchase of three extremely rare manuscripts that probably came from Alexandria. One was a very old Hebraic version of the New Testament, and another was a book of Plato's written in ancient Greek. When Còsimo feared that his death was imminent, he told Ficino to stop work on the first two manuscripts and to put all of his attention on the third, which he hoped to read before he died."

"So what was the third manuscript?" asked Chris expectantly.

"The third manuscript," Alicia explained," was a collection of sacred writings from ancient Egypt called the *Hermetica*."

"I'm pretty sure there was something with that name among the books discovered at Nag Hammadi," I said.

"What is the *Hermetica*?" asked Chris curiously.

"It's a collection of extraordinary mystical writings," Alicia replied. "The author is believed to be Thoth, the Egyptian god of magic and wisdom and founder of writing and geometry. The Greeks called him, *Hermes Trismegistus*, which means *Thrice Greatest*. He was believed to have been a contemporary of Moses—perhaps even his teacher. Thoth is represented in Egyptian art as having the body of a man and the head of an ibis."

"What was so important about this particular collection of texts that Còsimo Mèdici specifically wanted to read it before he died?" asked Chris.

"Well, while the Church Father, Clement of Alexandria, wrote extensively about the forty-two books of Hermes, only fragments of the *Hermetica* are still in existence," replied Alicia. "From what I understand, they describe how the soul, or the divine spark, that descended into matter, can throw off its attachments to the material world while still alive. It can then return to the realm of Light, having encountered a 'gnosis,' or direct realization of God."

"It sounds like the Cathar, don't you think?" I asked.

"It does," said Alicia. "But this idea of a direct realization of God causing a spiritual rebirth or resurrection is really, really old. It was conceptualized by the ancient Egyptians in their Isis and Osiris myth. Are you familiar with it?" she asked, almost as an afterthought.

"Not really," I said, as Chris and I waited for Alicia to go on.

"I'm not sure if I have this exactly right," said Alicia "But the great Egyptian god, Osiris, had a brother named Seth who was very jealous of him and plotted his murder. After carefully taking Osiris' measurements, Seth had an extraordinarily beautiful golden sarcophagus built. During a celebration at the god's palace, Seth invited everyone to lie inside the beautiful coffin to see who it would best fit. When Osiris took his turn, he, of course, fit perfectly. Before Osiris had a chance to get out, Seth quickly slammed the lid, sealed it with lead and then threw the beautiful coffin into the Nile.

"This murder is supposed to have taken place on January 17th, which, curiously, is a very important date at Rennes le Château, remember? It's the date that Marie Blanchefort died, the day Father Saunière had his stroke and the feast day of Saint Anthony."

"And the day Father Saunière's companion Marie died," I added.

"Is that just a coincidence?" asked Chris, who then looked back at me and acknowledged, "OK, you're right. It's unlikely to be a coincidence."

Alicia continued. "When Isis, the beloved wife of Osiris, learned of her husband's fate, she immediately set out, grief stricken, to find his body.

She did eventually find it, but then Seth stole it from her, and then cut Osiris' body up into fourteen pieces and scattered the pieces throughout the world. The result of Isis' subsequent search for her husband's remains produced only thirteen of the fourteen pieces.

"Thirteen, remember, is the number of great significance to the Templar. The fourteenth and missing piece turns out to be the phallus, which Isis, under the direction of Hermes Trismegistus, had reconstructed in gold.

"Once Isis reassembled (or *re-membered*, the word used in the story) the complete body of her husband, she and Osiris conceived a son and named him Horus. Horus represents the immortal, immaculately conceived, resurrected self that has *re-membered* its true nature, which is that of God.

"In Egyptian symbology, Isis has always represented these mysteries. She was very often depicted in the pre-Christian world seated alone on a throne, or seated on a throne with her immaculately conceived son, Horus, on her lap."

"It sounds to me as if you're describing the Virgin Mary with her child, Jesus, on her lap" I said.

"Or the Black Virgin," added Chris.

"Whatever you call her," said Alicia. "We still have the symbol, but the Church hijacked it as its own. What we no longer have is the knowledge of what the symbol represented, because according to orthodox Christianity, there was only one virgin birth, only one Resurrection and only one way to achieve salvation. If you even considered setting out on this path alone… well, you know what happened. But back in ancient, Egypt, these opportunities were available to everyone.

"Anyway, in terms of the *Hermetica*, from what I understand, it was one of the major inspirations for the Renaissance," Alicia continued, "and it created serious problems for all the great artists of Florence.

After Còsimo's death, his translator, Ficino, spent the greater part of his life trying to convince the Church authorities that the *Hermetica* could be reconciled with Christianity. While he was fairly effective in his endeavor, his successors were significantly less so.

Ficino's protégé, Giordano Bruno, who was less concerned with reconciling the *Hermetica's* teachings with the Church, became so bold as to declare the teachings of the *Hermetica* superior to Christianity. He was very vocal in his belief that Christianity had replaced the deeply spiritual tradition of the *Hermetica* by what he called *the worship of dead things, foolish rites, bad moral behavior and constant wars.* As you can imagine, Bruno was arrested by the Inquisition, tortured for eight years and eventually burned at the stake.

"So did Leonardo's problems with the Church also stem from this book, this *Hermetica?*" asked Chris.

"Maybe," Alicia replied. "Many people now believe that lots of his paintings contain symbolic representations of the ancient mysteries and secrets related to Jesus, and like Botticelli's, are occult talisman. Botticelli actually described one of his paintings as a '*talisman of occult* radiance' intended to magically inspire the viewer into an altered state of spiritual awareness. I do know for sure that Leonardo used the outlawed Pythagorean Golden Mean in the Mona Lisa. "

"Golden what?" I asked. "Didn't you tell me this Golden Mean was used at Rennes le Château in the construction of the Tower Magdala?"

"Right. The Golden Mean, I think, may have originated with Pythagoras. Plato was an initiate of his and their philosophies were both outlawed by the Church. The two of them are said to have received their mystical knowledge from Egypt and to have been *perfected* there," said Alicia.

"Perfected?" I asked. "Now that is definitely a connection with the Cathar."

"I think I'm lost?" said Chris, clearly puzzled by the sudden turn the conversation had taken. "Are you saying that the philosophy of Plato was outlawed by the Church?

"Plato's *Republic* was definitely among the collection of books hidden by the monks at Nag Hammadi," I contributed.

Alicia ignored Chris' question and turned to me, saying, "By the way, are you aware that the ancient Egyptians used the bee to symbolize Isis and her mysteries?"

"Well that certainly is a…" began Chris. But she didn't say the word.

After that no one said anything for a long time. It all seemed so tangled and so frustratingly twisted, I thought as I sat back and closed my eyes. And yet, maybe it's really not. Maybe it's our thinking that's been twisted by years of education and indoctrination by the Church. Maybe it's all really perfectly clear, and it's just we who can't see the truth.

The drive continued quite smoothly until it began to rain, and the traffic slowed down considerably. At first the rain was light, then became a torrential downpour. As the rain poured down and the driving conditions became hazardous, I started to feel anxious that we might not make it to Chartres that night. But then, a sign for our turnoff came into view.

Once we had turned off the *autoroute*, the rain slowed and soon we could see the towers of the cathedral of Chartres rising straight up from the fields of wheat and corn. Unlike any cathedral that we'd previously seen, Chartres, even through the clouds and rain, was an awe-inspiring sight. Nothing on the horizon could compete with it. For miles, we needed no maps or directions as the towering spires, solitary on the skyline, like a magnet, drew us in.

CHAPTER EIGHTEEN

The Mother Temple of the Lost Mysteries

> She is the paragon of all beauty.
> The reply to all desire.
> Whatever in the world has lured,
> whatever has seemed to promise joy,
> has been premonitory of her existence.
> For she is the incarnation of the promise of perfection.
> The soul's assurance that at the conclusion of its exile,
> the bliss that was known will be known again.
> To be initiated is to have the veils of ignorance torn away.
>
> Joseph Campbell, *The Hero with a Thousand Faces*

WE ARRIVED IN THE TOWN OF CHARTRES just as the sky had begun to fade to evening. The rain, which had turned quite cold, continued to fall as we searched for a hotel room. After making our selection surprisingly fast, we stashed our belongings in the tiny room. Then, we ran back out into the diminishing light hoping to get a closer look at what we had come to see.

As we crossed the street and approached the medieval cathedral, the three of us abruptly stopped. What stood in front of us completely dwarfed all our expectations. It was enormous. The ancient structure was massive beyond belief. And it was beautiful, far more beautiful than we'd ever imagined. Two spectacular towers of differing styles and heights, which nonetheless appeared perfectly harmoniously proportioned, soared above us. Immense pinnacles, elegant gables and spectacular stone steeples rose up in every direction.

The structure had an extraordinary, indescribable presence. It was immense, immediate and timeless. From the very moment I first set eyes on it, I knew without a shadow of doubt it would change me. In fact, I knew it would change all of us.

After settling ourselves down from the initial shock of our first encounter with Chartres, we proceeded up the stone stairs leading to the huge ancient wooden doors. While we found them secured for the night, we never for a moment felt shut out. In fact, it seemed oddly as if Chartres had been waiting, waiting patiently for us to arrive.

Oblivious to the cold rain penetrating our clothing after finding the building closed, our attention was drawn to the elongated stone figures carved into the cathedral's facade. In our explorations of religious buildings we had seen a great deal of medieval stone sculpture, much of which had been quite beautiful. But the sculpture on Chartres' Western Door, known in the Middle Ages as the Pilgrim's Gate, could not be compared to anything we'd seen before.

Like performers in a play, the expressive, lifelike stone figures of ancient Judaic queens and Old Testament prophets and patriarchs stood crowned and dressed in their swirling royal robes, seemingly extending a personal welcome to us.

The sensitive figures held mysterious stone scrolls, their eyes revealing a timeless knowing, their hands raised and poised to express, all hinting at what awaited us on the other side of the mighty doors.

Eventually, the demands of our bodies for dry clothes, food and sleep could no longer be ignored. Reluctantly we turned away. After a simple meal next to a warm fire in a cozy restaurant across from the cathedral we went back to our hotel room and immediately collapsed into our beds. With very little to say to each other, we easily drifted off to sleep beneath the shadows of Chartres' spires. And of course, I dreamed that night of the girl from Montségur. As usual, she was running in front of me, her hair trailing behind her in the wind.

Waking up early the following morning, Alicia, Chris and I shared a common but unspoken sense of nervous expectation as we rushed about bumping into each other in the small hotel room. While no one spoke the words, it was clear that each of us secretly expected the Gothic cathedral of Chartres to explain everything.

The rain had stopped during the night and the sun was shining. Once dressed, we hurried out into the cold morning air like eager children on Christmas morning. Barely aware of anything else in the bustling town, now alive in activity, we ran across the street and up the stairs to Chartres' Western Portal. This time we found it unlocked.

As we pushed open the immense doors and moved from the early morning sunlight into the strange illuminated blue darkness of the cathedral, I immediately lost my footing and literally fell into the enormous enclosure. For the next several seconds, I was unable to shake the sensation that I was falling. The amazing light, the enormity of the space, the indescribable uplifting movement all prevented me for some time from establishing a secure contact with the ground.

When I eventually regained some semblance of balance and adjusted my eyes to the unusual opalescent light, I saw in front of me a dazzling world of fantastic impossibilities.

It was absolutely astonishing! Unimaginable! Huge walls of jeweled colored glass seemed to be supporting the most massive walls I'd ever seen. Spectacular cylindrical stone columns of unbelievable girth gracefully lifted the enormous structure into space, seeming to disregard completely every law of gravity.

While the architecture seemed to be amazingly complex, twisting and turning, rising and crossing, there was at the same time a striking sense of coherence, unity and wholeness. And as virtually all my senses were set a buzz in stimulation, I concurrently felt a deep spiritual calm unlike anything I'd ever felt before.

I looked to Alicia and Chris for confirmation that I had not drifted off into one of my strange dreamlike states. "Are the two of you seeing what I'm seeing?" I asked them.

Their astounded expressions assured me that, in fact, they were. Slowly, still uncertain of my own footing while we bathed in the indescribable blue light, we allowed Chartres to draw us into its immense nave. We shook our heads in wonder as we moved more deeply into the building and up the main aisle toward the altar. I had to keep looking down at my feet to constantly assure myself that, contrary to what I was feeling, they remained securely on the ground.

Shortly, we found ourselves crossing into the transept of the cathedral, the very center of the building where all three entryways converged. At this point, as if instinctively, the three of us stopped and turned around to face the direction from which we had just come. Blazing above the Western Door was an enormous Rose Window that appeared to be revolving like a shimmering pinwheel in the wind. The spinning, sparkling, jewel-like, explosion of pulsating color suspended in the blue darkness once again caused me to lose my balance.

"It's in the West," said Alicia, "to symbolize the setting sun and the end of time. See? Everything's designed in a sequence of 12, the number of completion. And look," she said pointing to the left, "there's the Egyptian after-world court of Osiris. See the scales?"

I strained to make out what she was pointing to, but I was still far too dizzy. "How are you able to focus on anything other than whirling circles?" I asked. "I feel as if I'm looking through a kaleidoscope."

But a few minutes later, I began to be able to distinguish some angels blowing trumpets, and eventually I could see shrouded individuals coming up out of tombs.

"So if twelve is completion," I whispered to myself more than to anyone else, "does thirteen, the Templar's favorite number, symbolize resurrection?"

"According to my book," said Chris "It's a complex *invisible geometry* that creates the effect of movement. But this glass," she continued, "was actually made with real gold and jewels and no one has ever been able to figure out how it was done. A few other cathedrals have glass that was made here in the glazier workshop at Chartres. But once Chartres was finished, the workshop was closed up and no glass like it has ever been seen again."

I wasn't sure what Chris meant by *invisible geometry*. I was sure, however, that these windows were incredibly beautiful and touched my heart in a way I could not explain.

Above both the north and south entrances were equally astounding Rose Windows. But the Rose to the North was of most interest to us. By the time we had turned to face in its direction, I had regained my balance and my ability to focus. And there at the center of the North Rose sat an enthroned and decidedly Black Virgin and Child.

"It's the Black Virgin!" Chris gasped.

"Or is it Isis?" asked Alicia.

There were five lancets beneath the Black Virgin, and on the far left was a crowned king holding a stone above a chalice.

"It says here," said Chris, "that the king with the chalice is Melchizedek."

"Yes, there's a book in the outlawed *Nag Hammadi Gospels* attributed to him," I recalled.

Next to Melchizedek was David holding his harp, and next to David, his son, King Solomon, the builder of the great Temple of Jerusalem holding his mason tools. Next to Solomon was Aaron, the brother of Moses.

"Look, Aaron's wearing the twelve-jeweled bronze vest the Merovingians gave to St. Rémy, the bishop that baptized the Merovingian king Clovis," I exclaimed.

"Is it possible," asked Alicia, "that we're looking at a line of initiates, the true, anointed succession of *Brides and Bridegrooms?*"

The center lancet beneath the North Rose depicted a mother and child that, according to Chris' guidebook, was Saint Anne. The child she held in her lap was identified as the Virgin Mary. Anne's face was strangely veiled in black, with only her eyes visible.

"What does your book say about why she's veiled?" I asked Chris.

"I can't find any mention of it at all," replied Chris. "But it does say that the North Rose Window and its lancets used to be collectively known as the Initiate Window."

We crossed the transept again and began to walk along the south aisle, looking briefly at the windows as we continued. I was amazed by the light in the building. It was an illumination unlike anything I'd ever seen before. How could it be so dark and yet so light at the same time?

The light must change, I imagined, every hour of every day and every day throughout the year.

Our walk brought us into Chartres' ambulatory and past some of the cathedral's greatest treasures. On the south side of the building was one of the oldest and most famous windows, *Notre-Dame-de-la-Belle-Verriere, Our Mother of the Beautiful Window*. On the north was Chartres' prized relic, the *Sancta Camisia,* a piece of what is believed to have been a silken veil once belonging to the Virgin Mary.

Encased in a reliquary of glass and gold, the *Camisia,* according to Chris' guidebook, had been passed down by Charlemagne and brought to Chartres in 876 by his grandson, King Charles the Bald. As we walked, the ancient architecture continued to astound us as the remarkable stone twisted and turned above our heads "I don't understand," said Chris, interrupting our silent observations. "Somebody please explain this to me. This is a Catholic Church, isn't it? Where's Jesus? I haven't even seen one single crucifix?"

"I think we're in a Temple of the Mother," I said.

"I think we're in a Temple of the great Mother Goddess," said Alicia. "It's the Temple of Isis and of the lost mysteries of resurrection and rebirth."

Eventually, we came to a small chapel where a statue of a dark-skinned woman holding a scepter in one hand and a symbol of the world in the other, stood at the center. Crowned and richly dressed in white satin and gold brocade, the black statue was bordered on either side by hundreds of flickering candles. Above her head was an illuminated canopy decorated with rows of golden hearts. Crystal chandeliers, the only electric lights I'd seen in the entire cathedral, illuminated the little chapel in a soft eerie glow.

"It's another Black Virgin," whispered Chris.

"She's so sweet," breathed Alicia.

As we stood in this lovely little chapel, my eyes unexpectedly filled with tears. I sat down on one of the chairs in front of the Black Virgin and Alicia and Chris sat down beside me.

For some reason, as we sat in front of the beautiful Black Virgin I found I could no longer hold inside all the sadness and loss I'd experienced over the past few months. It just seemed to pour out of me, unbidden and unbridled.

I'd completely lost faith in the Church, in its traditions and teachings and most of all in its fundamental goodness. I'd lost forever the sacred stories of my childhood and along with them, the simple joys of Christmas and Easter. I'd lost the place I had felt rooted, the place where I'd found meaning and had innocently trusted.

Now, I felt ignorant, naive and cynical. Perhaps worst of all, I'd lost my connection to anything soulful and to everything sacred. But sitting in the presence of the beautiful Black Virgin, in the flickering candlelight, surrounded by the incredible blue luminescence of Chartres, I felt the darkness beginning to lift and the shadows to clear.

After awhile, when there wasn't a single tear left inside of me, I dried my face on my sleeve and stood up. Alicia and Chris stood up as well and the three of us silently continued our walk through the magical cathedral of Chartres.

On the north side of the building, we came upon a small group of women who appeared to be lining up for something. Noticing that they were speaking English to each other, we questioned them and learned that they were preparing to embark on a guided tour of the cathedral's crypt. Immediately we decided to join them and hurried, as they instructed us, to buy our tickets in the cathedral's bookshop. By the time we had returned, the tour was ready to begin.

Our tour guide led us through a roped off passageway and down a flight of stone stairs. As we descended into the dark musty stillness of the subterranean crypt, the temperature dropped about twenty degrees. From the fiery-jeweled splendor of the cathedral above, we suddenly entered an underground enclosure that felt like a mythic underworld, a lightless cave or an ancient tomb.

"We're in the womb of the cathedral," Alicia whispered.

It was cold and strange, and most of all, dark. Our guide directed our immediate attention to a beautiful twelfth century fresco. He explained that the fresco represented Charlemagne asking the bishop of Chartres to forgive a sin committed by his grandfather, Charles Martel.

"It was for a sin so great," the tour guide specified, "that Charles Martel was never able to confess it himself."

"Humph! It was a grave sin, all right," said one of the British women to her companions. "It was Charles Martel who assisted the Church in breaking its sacred oath with the Merovingians. The ancient mysteries could have been lost forever."

Alicia, Chris and I looked at each other wide-eyed, but then were quickly rushed through the narrow tunnel-like passage. Our guide spoke as he hurried us along, explaining the history of the cathedral. "The crypt of Chartres was built in 1020." he said, "But Chartres has been the site of a Christian church since the fourth century, and known as a sacred place of worship for centuries earlier. The first bishop of record to preside over the diocese of Chartres," he continued, "was Valentinus in the early fourth century."

I remembered that several texts in the Nag Hammadi collection of outlawed books had been attributed to someone named Valentinus. Later, I had learned that he had been a disciple of St. Paul's, but was for some reason considered a dangerous heretic by the Church. It seemed quite unusual that a bishop would be named after a famous heretic, but then again, there was nothing usual about the cathedral of Chartres.

Our tour guide interrupted my thoughts. "The ancient priests of the Celts called the Druids came to worship at Chartres once a year, centuries before there was a cathedral here," he explained. "They believed it was a sacred place and a point of very high energy, the highest point of energy in their entire kingdom. A place where the Goddess intervened."

Before I could ask a question about Druids and high energy, however, our tour guide rushed us along. Suddenly, I felt Chris grab hold of my hand, "Slow down," she whispered, pointing in the direction of the British group who had slowed their pace and were speaking to one another. I motioned to Alicia and we all stopped to hear what was being said.

"Over a thousand years ago, a giant stone stood on this mound, called a *dolmen*," said the same woman who'd just made the comment about the Merovingians. "The *dolmen's* purpose was to accumulate, amplify and direct the intense currents underneath the earth. The master builders of Chartres understood the ancient science, and magnified the currents further to awaken from their deep sleep of the flesh, those who came to Chartres to be *perfected*."

My heart skipped a beat hearing the word *perfected*. "We're losing the other guide and the rest of the group," Chris whispered as she pointed down the long narrow vault. When we had once again caught up, our guide was leading the group into the chapel of the crypt.

There were no decorations in this chapel, no color and very little light. But beneath the low, barrel-vaulted ceilings in the very front of the chapel was a small altar. In the place of honor was what the guide called *Notre-Dame-de-Sous-Terre,* meaning *Our Lady Under the Earth.* It was another Black Virgin!

The guide explained that she was only a modern copy of the Druid's *Virgini Pariturae,* the Virgin about to give birth, which had been destroyed during the Revolution.

"She is the goddess, the one whom some say it's best not to name," we heard the British woman whisper to her group. "Some call her Isis, and she is black because she represents the tradition of the Great Mysteries as they were once celebrated along the Nile."

The guide was hurrying us on again. Wait! I wanted to say. I want to hear more!

But then the group of British women closed in on themselves, making it clear that their conversation was private, and the guide rushed us onward to Chartres' ancient well.

One by one, the members of the group approached the small well and stared down into the bottomless blackness. The guide explained that the well's water, which was about 130 feet beneath the surface, had long been believed to possess tremendous healing powers.

When it was the British group's turn to observe the well, Chris, Alicia and I moved in close to hear what they would say.

"Baptismal cleansing in the sacred water of Chartres' well was a central rite of the Mysteries," the British woman told her group. "The water from this well readied the initiate for resurrection. Its special properties awoke the soul from the sleep of materiality, from the forgetfulness of the flesh. In the gospel are stories about how John the Baptist performed this ritual cleansing on Jesus. But it is only up to this point that the teachings of the Church can take you. The path forward has been hidden. Once cleansed," the woman added, "the initiate was given honey to revitalize the immortal self."

Honey? I wondered. Is this a connection with the bees? Did they help revitalize the immortal self? Again, after we had observed the well, we were hurried up a flight of stairs.

"Sadly, most who come here will walk away having seen nothing more than a beautiful building," said the woman to her group as they walked up the stairs behind us. "But now I will show you the two ibis drinking from the Grail Cup, the signature of Hermes Trismegistus, scribe of the mysteries that have been carefully hidden here at Chartres for all those who have eyes to see."

Now, having climbed up from the very depths of darkness in the crypt, we found ourselves suddenly outside in the jarring light of day. The British woman turned and led her group back into the cathedral.

Chris, Alicia and I looked at each other, each clearly fascinated by all we just heard on our tour of Chartres' crypt. But the crisp winter air felt invigorating, and rather than go back inside the cathedral as we saw the British group doing, we decided to walk Chartres' perimeter.

Alicia and Chris wanted to talk but I felt a pressing need to be alone and silent. So I dropped back behind the two of them and decided to take some pictures of Chartres' exterior.

As I took my camera from around my neck and removed my lens cap, I heard Alicia say that Osiris, Mithra and Dionysus had all been born in caves, and that according to the gospel of either Matthew or Mark, she wasn't sure which, so had Jesus.

I didn't listen any further but instead began focusing my telephoto lens on the external architecture of Chartres. Almost right away I noticed that I was feeling that curious sense of awareness that came over me sometimes.

Without trying to understand what was happening, I just focused my camera lens on the twisting, turning and soaring lines of the enormous building. As I felt my concentration fix more and more deeply, I began to perceive a slight movement in the stone. It wasn't exactly that the stone was moving... it was more like I was seeing a radiant energy moving through it.

And then, barely perceptible at first, there was a humming or whir-ring sound. Where was it coming from? I called to Alicia and Chris, but they were too far away to hear me and too engrossed in their conversation to notice. When I came to a point of the building where I could see the astonishing flying buttresses clearly, I gasped. Now not only could I see and hear the energy moving through the stone, but as it moved through the flying buttresses, it was throwing off brilliant, multicolored sparks.

Seconds later I began to actually feel the radiant energy of Chartres moving through the inside of my own body. All at once, I felt as if a thin line of molten lava was racing up my spine and exploding into sunbursts of color in my head.

I steadied myself and then called out louder to my friends, "Look at this! Look at these flying buttresses! You can actually feel this energy!" Deep in conversation, my friends looked over at me, nodded and then returned to their discussion.

"No, no!" I called back to them. "I mean, really look at these flying buttresses, they're amazing! Do you see the sparks of color? Aren't they fantastic?"

Alicia and Chris finally looked at me. Then they looked back at each other and burst out laughing. "Yes, yes, the flying buttresses are beautiful!" they both called out. But I knew that no one but I had seen or felt the powerful, hidden energies of Chartres.

CHAPTER NINETEEN

Through the Labyrinth

At the threshold of understanding an unexpected price is require.

Thomas Moore, *Care of the Soul*

MY UNUSUAL "SEEING" NORMALIZED once we were back into the hustle and bustle of activity around the main entrance of the cathedral. While Alicia and Chris continued their conversation, I overheard a group of American students standing next to us discussing the view from one of the towers of Chartres.

"Is it possible to go up there?" I asked them.

"Yes," the students replied. "The view is really cool!"

"I'm tired and don't do well with heights," said Chris. "I don't think I want to go up there. You two go ahead, and I'll wait for you down here."

"Oh, come on," I said. "From up there we'll be able to see so much more of the architecture."

"Let's do," said Alicia to Chris. "And then we'll call it a day."

We were soon climbing the narrow stone steps up the cathedral's North Tower. "If I get sick," warned Chris as we climbed, "I'll blame it on the two of you."

The stonework on the stairway of the North Tower was remarkable, each stone beautifully carved in intricate designs and patterns.

"I wonder how many medieval pilgrims actually made this climb?" I asked.

"Probably not many," said Alicia. "Maybe only the person who rang the bells came up this high."

"And yet," said Chris, "it looks as if every stone, even those way up here, were given as much attention as those that were part of the main altar. Why would the builders do that?"

"I was just thinking the same thing," said Alicia, "It looks as if every block of stone is someone's masterpiece. It's almost as if the actual construction of the building itself was a spiritual exercise."

Climbing still higher in the tower, we came upon the fantastic gargoyles that the medieval builders believed protected their sacred buildings from negative forces. Then, from the amazing vantage point of the balcony, we began wondering about the building in ways we hadn't previously.

During the tour we'd learned that the Gothic cathedral of Chartres had been built in only thirty years. Now, standing on the balcony of the North Tower, this information no longer seemed believable. How had this massive work of art been constructed in only thirty years? Who had built it? And where had this extraordinary architectural form come from?

And there were more questions. How had the workers raised the huge stone blocks to these astounding heights? How had the colossal project been funded? And who had provided the otherworldly stained glass?

Gazing down from the top of the tower, as the wind wound around the elegant spires and whipped through our hair, we doubted we'd ever find any logical answers to our questions.

We climbed down in silence, Chartres having stripped away once again our ability to speak. After descending the tower, we found ourselves wandering among the sculptured columns on the North Porch. Suddenly, a gasp from Chris drew our attention. "Look at this!" she pointed. Carved on a badly damaged column was a scene that appeared to depict the Ark of the Covenant being pulled on wheels by two oxen. A carving on the adjacent column showed a man standing in the middle of a mound of dead bodies covering the Ark with a veil.

There was another man in this carving who appeared to be a medieval knight, dressed in a full coat of mail, his spear penetrating one of the fallen bodies. At the bottom of the column was a Latin inscription that we tried, but were unable, to read.

"It looks like a medieval knight fighting for possession of the Ark of the Covenant, doesn't it?" asked Chris. "Over here," she said, pointing to the next scene, "he's hiding it and carrying it away."

"Is he a Templar?" asked Alicia.

"How would I know?" sighed Chris, exasperated by the question. "Maybe it's time to go home."

"Oh, but we can't go yet," said Alicia. "We've totally forgotten the Labyrinth."

"Labyrinth?" I asked.

"But we agreed we'd leave after the tower," Chris reminded Alicia.

"The Labyrinth is an ancient symbol of the path of initiation and walking it was an important part of the medieval pilgrimage to Chartres," said Alicia. "We have to do it."

Chris and I reluctantly agreed and we reentered the building through the door on the North Porch, which our guidebook said in the Middle Ages had been called the Initiate's Door.

Back inside the building in the darkness of the magical blue light, we found the Labyrinth painted on the stones of the floor in the shadow of the West Rose Window. Surprisingly, most of the Labyrinth was covered over with chairs which explained why we hadn't seen it earlier. Alicia explained that medieval pilgrims from all over the world came to Chartres each year on the summer solstice to walk the entire Labyrinth in their bare feet.

In keeping with tradition, we removed our shoes and began making our way through the spiral path of the Labyrinth maneuvering between the chairs as we walked. The cold stone felt soothing to my tired feet.

"Why did they come on the solstice?" asked Chris.

"It was a day sacred to the Druids, the magician-priests of the ancient Celts who worshiped here at Chartres long before the Christians," replied Alicia. "It's also the day of the year with the most light. I think the Druids considered light a materialization of God. I've read that the center stone in the Labyrinth marks the highest energy point in the cathedral. Let's stand on it!"

We dutifully marched towards it, but when we had located the center stone, we discovered that a barefoot woman with her eyes closed was already standing on it. We waited somewhat impatiently until she had moved away. Then all three of us hurried to the spot and huddled together.

Whether from all the walking we'd been doing that day, or because I was just very tired, my knees started trembling almost immediately. Looking up, I noticed in surprise that Alicia and Chris were both trembling, as well. Seconds later, all three of us collapsed onto nearby chairs.

Before we'd had a chance to collect ourselves or to figure out what was going on, the woman who'd been standing on the stone approached us. Dressed in a dark, very somber suit, her salt-and-pepper-colored hair arranged neatly in a tight chignon at the back of her head, the woman gazed directly at us.

"Are you aware of what you're doing?" she demanded in heavily accented but perfect English. Before I had a chance to even consider a response, Chris had elbowed Alicia and me aside and shot back, "Yes, we are."

I'd never before heard Chris speak with such authority. I was startled by her bold response and very curious to see what she would say next.

"Tell me, then," continued the woman. "What are your reasons for standing on that particular stone?" The sound of her voice was that of a strict schoolmarm, and her body language actually bordered on intimidation.

Alicia and I both turned to Chris. "Underneath our feet," Chris said unhesitatingly, "is the highest energy point in the building. We're standing here to experience the benefits of the uplifting, healing forces."

"Ah, so you do know some of the secrets of Chartres," the woman replied, a half-smile slowly warming her face. The tension in her body relaxed. "Do you also know that you must be very careful not to stand on the powerful Labyrinth stone for too long?"

"Too long?" asked Chris, softening her tone as well.

"I take the train from Paris once a month to stand on this spot for fifteen minutes at a time," explained the woman. "At first I could only stand on the stone for less than a minute. I began coming here after both my lungs had collapsed and my surgeon in Germany had told me he could offer no further help. His final advice to me was to come to this stone at Chartres."

"And has it helped?" asked Chris. "Has your health improved?"

"Oh, yes!" she replied. "It's not only the energy beneath our feet that is powerful at this point. The healing blue light from the windows converges here and the vaulted ceiling amplifies it. The building was actually designed to create a healing energy field right on this exact spot. Very few people that come to Chartres however know about this. In fact, most of the people who come to Chartres simply regard it as another beautiful building or another architectural wonder. But it is so much more."

Fascinated by her revelations, we listened without interrupting as she continued. "In the Middle Ages people, sick people from all over Europe walked to Chartres to bathe in the water of the well down in the crypt. They would also stand on this spot to be washed in the healing blue light. But it was not only those looking for physical healing who came to Chartres. It was those seeking to be *perfected*."

There was that word again! The Cathar had used it to identify those who had received the sacrament of the *consolamentum*. Was it possible that Chartres had something to do with the Cathar? I wanted to ask but I didn't want to interrupt or to say anything that might scare the woman on the Labyrinth away. I knew by now that meeting her was no simple coincidence.

The woman sighed and then sat down on a chair next to us. None of us said a word. We just waited, hoping she would go on.

"So many come to this life," she continued, "as if to a festival. They come to buy, and to sell, and to compete in the various games that are offered. But there are a few, a chosen few, who come into this incarnation with a shadowy memory of being part of something greater. These select few always somehow find their way to Chartres."

I suddenly remembered the Latin inscription we'd just seen beneath the carving of the Ark on the column of the North Door. I whispered in Chris' ear, "Ask her if she knows the meaning of the Latin words carved on the column."

"You mean the White Knight's Column?" the woman asked in response to Chris' question.

"Do you know the translation of the Latin?" Chris pressed.

"Look over there," the woman suddenly directed. She pointed to the familiar *crèche* set up on an altar in one of Chartres' chapels, still on display since Christmas. The usual components were present: the Virgin Mary, her husband Joseph, the three wise men, the baby Jesus, the shepherds and the various barnyard animals.

"It's a nice story, isn't it?" she asked. "It's pleasant. It makes people happy. Unfortunately, it's not the real story."

We nodded our agreement,

"The Virgin birth, in the language of the mysteries, signifies transcendental rebirth, the central experience of initiation. This symbol was never intended to be translated literally. *Except a man be born again,* the initiate John tells us, *he can not enter the kingdom of God.*

"The immaculately conceived, bachelor god man, Jesus of Nazareth, was the invention of a Roman Emperor and a fourth century council of bishops," she continued. "The story was assembled with hijacked bits and pieces of the ancient mystery traditions put to use in the service of the new state religion, Christianity."

"Are you talking about the Council of Nicea?" asked Alicia.

"I am," the woman replied. "Constantine and his bishops took what they could use for their new misogynist cult of the cross from the ancient pathway of perfection, its rites and rituals and its transcendent symbols. What they didn't want, such as the Divine Feminine, they outlawed on penalty of death. The mystical significance of the Virgin Birth, the Resurrection, the Mystical Supper and the Giving of the Head was soon lost in the shadows to all but a very few."

The Giving of the Head? I wondered. Could this have something to do with the human skull sitting next to Mary Magdalene in all the depictions of her at Rennes le Château? Or with the skull and crossbones on the Templar Knight's flag?

I exchanged a questioning glance with Chris, but neither of us spoke.

The woman continued. "On the path of the mysteries the Resurrection had always been available to any who sought it. But by the twelfth century," she said, "the ancient tradition was under the protection of only a handful of loyal noble families. This pathway to *perfection,* the tradition of Moses handed down to Jesus and his initiate wife Mary Magdalene, who anointed him as the Christ and became his sister bride, had survived millenniums.

"But now its scared treasures and records were being threatened by complete extinction. Bernard of Clairvaux, a guardian of the mysteries by birth, understood the dire state of affairs and under the patronage of the powerful Count of Champagne organized an emergency rescue mission to the Holy Lands to recover the sacred Ark of the Covenant.

"The Ark of the Covenant?" interrupted Alicia. "Wasn't the Ark just a container for the Ten Commandments? What do the Ten Commandments have to do with the Mysteries?"

"The Ark is not what is generally supposed," the woman explained. "In the sculpture, the ark is veiled to indicate concern with its secret nature. It was actually designed by the hierophant Moses following his initiation in Egypt. Its esoteric purpose was to protect sacred scripture and records as well as mystical objects such as the secret Table of Testimony, the precise harmonic principles of measurement and proportion required to build a sanctuary for the Shekinah, like Chartres."

"The Shekinah?" asked Chris.

"She is the Divine Feminine, Protectress of the Mysteries. You might know her as Isis, or as the Black Virgin, as the Magdalene or as Notre Dame de Chartres," the woman replied.

At this point, she paused, but as none of us said anything, she soon began again. "And yes, I know the translation at the North Door," she continued. "It says, *Here things take their course. You are to work through the Ark*. Do you understand?"

"Not exactly," replied Chris, speaking for the three of us.

"After the Knights returned to France," she said, "under the direction of Bernard, they built Chartres according to the ways of the ancient initiate builders. Here at Chartres, under the protection of the Black Virgin, on the mound of the sacred stone of the Druids, they preserved the ancient path of the mysteries.

"This building is an initiate's encyclopedia of knowledge. It is a library of ancient wisdom. There are others built in this magical tradition, but there are none like Chartres. The signature of these builders is a ray of light directed to a specific point in the building on a specific day of the year. The sanctuary of Montségur is signed in this way as are other of the Cathar sanctuaries in the Pyrénées.

"Montségur ?" I blurted out incredulously. "The Cathar?"

"Of course," the woman confirmed. "The path of Jesus, the Magdalene's path was the same ancient path of the Cathar. This was the treasure they would not allow to be burned in the fires of the Church. They knew for certain that others would come later seeking the pathway and they under-stood it must be preserved whatever the cost."

I felt an ache in my heart at the thought of the peaceful Cathar of beautiful Occitania. I remembered the lovely and proud Esclarmonde de Foix, the brave young Raymond Robert Trencavel of Carcassonne, and Giralda de Lavaur who had been so brutally raped and then thrown down a well with her hands tied behind her back.

I thought of all of the gentle people who had been forced to give up their lives to preserve the ancient tradition so that seven hundred years later Alicia, Chris and I could find it. Or had it found us?

Suddenly appearing exhausted, the woman stopped speaking and stood up. "Well, that's enough," she said wearily. "I must go now. I have a train to catch. I am on my way to Germany to meet the Saunière family. Do you know of them?"

Of course we did. How amazing that this woman would be meet-ing the family of the village priest of Rennes le Château. Or on second thought, maybe it was not amazing at all. Maybe it made perfect sense. It was Father Saunière, the priest at Rennes le Château who had engaged in all the bizarre building projects in the village, including the especially bizarre renovation of the Church of Saint Mary Magdalene with all of its cryptic riddles.

The three of us nodded, totally at a loss for words.

"You have been to Rennes le Château?" she asked. "Do you remember the bas-relief of Mary Magdalene on the altar in the front in the church? The Magdalene is shown kneeling in front of a branch with two shoots, one that lives and one that has shriveled and died. The dead shoot repre-sents the Church of Rome that can take you nowhere. The shoot that lives represents the ancient sacred mysteries that she carried with her family to the south of France."

Speechless, we watched the woman on the Labyrinth prepare to leave. "I must go now," she said definitively. "The invisible path of the mysteries has brought you here. Now you must follow it. Continue to watch for its signs and symbols and you will never find yourself alone"

Signs and symbols, I thought as images of salamanders and bees came to mind.

"Those who follow the way," she concluded, "will find themselves and in themselves, God. Goodbye, and may your quest be blessed." And with that, the woman on the Labyrinth collected her purse and umbrella, then turned and walked away through the nave and toward the great Western Door.

The three of us sat there in stunned silence, attempting to digest all we had just heard. Alicia suddenly jumped up. "We can't just let her leave without knowing how to find her again. Go after her, Chris. Get her address or her phone number or something. We don't even know her name. We can't just let her leave!!"

But we did. We just stood there and watched as she retrieved a small suitcase on wheels from the cathedral bookshop and then pulled it out through the Western Door.

After awhile, we rose from our own seats and silently followed each other up the nave. As we moved toward the door, Chris pointed up to a window on the left side of the building, "It's the Magdalene window," she said, "There she is with her companions disembarking from their boat on the shores of France. And look! It's her brother, Lazarus, being raised from the dead and other shrouded figures coming up out of tombs, as well!"

CHAPTER TWENTY

The Conclusion

> For she comes as a messenger to remind us of our real origin and
> call us to become free again, to show how to make the journey
> not to some happy human state but to something far vaster. She
> is confronting us, if we can only learn to understand it, with the
> strangest prospect of all, the death of our own mortality.
>
> Peter Kingsley, *Reality*

WE LEFT CHARTRES late in the afternoon and arrived back in
Toulouse about midnight. Chris and Alicia dropped me at my front gate
and then quickly hurried off. As I sleepily made my way to the door, I was
struck by the brilliance of the stars in the midnight sky. Though the air
was quite chilly and I was exhausted, I stopped and leaned on one of the
old oak trees bordering the path to the house and gazed up.

Standing beneath the immense, sparkling dome, I remembered Chris
reading a description of Gothic architecture from her guidebook on the
way home. The book described Gothic as an *architecture of light.* As I
stood in the glimmering starlight, having only hours ago experienced the
celestial illumination of Chartres, the allusion I had missed previously
became perfectly clear.

So often in the past I had read histories of ancient peoples who were
said to worship the Light. They were always disparaged by the authors who

referred to them as *primitive* and as having been part of an archaic, imply-ing naive, *solar cult*. Now I understood that Light was simply a symbol for the world of the non-material, the world of the eternal.

Looking up at the awe-inspiring illumination above me, dwarfed by its dazzling wonder, I agreed that indeed Light was a perfect symbol for the most profound mysteries of life. As I once again began my walk down the path toward the door I realized that all the confusion, frustration and fear that I had experienced during the past several months had lifted.

Now, I felt only a deep calm. If I had only been able to trust my own internal directives, I thought, I would have spared myself so much discomfort.

If only I had recognized from the beginning that I was being guided along an ancient invisible path of an initiatory tradition that had been protected throughout time by the Great Mother.

If only I had known that I was being led to a secret treasure of unimag-ined value, a treasure guarded by the Merovingians, the Cathar, the Templar Knights, the great artists of the Renaissance and Father Saunière, the village priest of Rennes Le Château.

My journey had taken me through many twists and turns. But while almost everything I had been taught about Christianity—my own religious tradition—had fallen apart piece by piece, I had never considered that what I was losing was actually making room for something of far greater value. I'd had no idea that hidden behind the shadows of what I now under-stood to be the misogynist religious doctrine of a power seeking Church, behind the lifeless symbols and nonsensical stories I'd been instructed in as a child and taught to believe and not question, there had existed an ancient Western mystical tradition of Light that had been embraced by the most respected minds of Western Civilization.

I now believed that Christianity, along with the other great Western religious traditions, had actually served to separate people from themselves, from each other and most importantly from the recognition that everyone, despite their gender, ethnicity, sexual orientation, or religious affiliation has access to their own individual enlightenment, their own Resurrection. At least for the moment anyway, it now all seemed perfectly clear

By the time I had closed the front door behind me, I remembered the famous passage from the New Testament where Jesus described himself as the *Way, the Truth and the Light.*

Was this passage, I wondered, from the gospel of the Beloved Disciple, whom the Church identified as John? I now believed without a shadow of doubt that the true Beloved Disciple was the one who rested on Jesus' lap in Leonardo da Vinci's painting, *The Last Supper*—Mary Magdalene.

Sighing deeply, I went into the house. Everyone had already been asleep for hours but I stopped in each of the kids' bedrooms to kiss them goodnight and to pull the covers up around them. Rachel offered me a sleepy, "Hi, Mom."

Nicholas did the same, and then he pulled the covers off that I had just pulled up around him.

I was exhausted, but as I prepared myself for bed my mind continued to survey where my adventure had led me. Many questions still remained about the ancient tradition of the mysteries. What I was sure of was that the Church of Rome was not the tradition of Jesus, its popes, bishops and priests not its initiates. I knew for certain now that, unlike the Church, the true path of Jesus and his wife Mary Magdalene must be traveled alone.

The path to its mysteries, I now understood was one, that like the quest for the Holy Grail, must be tread alone, a path that could be followed only by developing trust in one's own individual inner directives. It was also clear to me that while the Catholic Church had stopped at nothing to suppress the tradition of the ancient mysteries and the families that protected it, the tradition had lived on.

There was no question in my mind that I had been directed to the medieval heretics, the Cathar. My visit to their sanctuary at Montségur had served as my own initiation into the ancient mysteries, awakening within me a Light that, once revealed, would not allow me to sleep.

Similarly, my encounter with the Cathar girl and her continued presence in my dreams had directed me on to the royal Merovingians, the Templar Knights, and finally to the true identity of the Magdalene.

By the time I had climbed into my own warm bed next to Bill, I could barely keep my eyes open. I was asleep as soon as I put my head down on the pillow.

It seemed that after having just closed my eyes, however, I began to dream. There she was, the girl from Montségur, my companion throughout my entire journey. As always, she ran ahead of me. This time, however, the dream was different than it had been in the past. This time the girl stopped, turned around, looked directly at me and spoke. While her lips never moved I understood exactly what she said to me.

"Each age has its witnesses," she said. "Those who have experienced the Light on the mountain must leave an illumination on the path so that others may follow."

Then she began to run. But as she did, she turned back once more to me and said, "When you are ready, we will go on."

I was awake immediately and could feel the anxiety rising and beginning to burn inside me. Go on? Go on where?

Then I caught myself. OK, I thought. We'll go on. While I didn't know where we'd be going, I did know that I would not be alone on my journey. I knew with a certainty gained only by direct experience that I would be guided to open hidden doors that had not yet been opened, to discover more secrets of the ancient mysteries that had been veiled in shadow throughout the past two thousand years.

I knew as well that as the Light continued to pour into my life, I would hold in my mind the image of both the salamander, with its capacity to move through the fire unharmed, and of the honeybee, symbolic of the sweetness of life's magnificent adventure.

Afterward

> The time will come when the secret wisdom
> shall once again be the dominating religious and philosophical urge
> of the world. Out of the cold ashes of lifeless creeds,
> shall rise phoenix like the ancient mysteries.
>
> Manly P. Hall, *The Secret Teachings of All Ages*

AS HAU TI LONG MOVED silently around my body inserting acupuncture needles, she did something she rarely did. She spoke.

"What do you do for a living?" she asked.

I had come to Hau on the recommendation of my good friend, Martha, following medical treatments that had left me feeling as if I had been impaled—which in fact, I had.

I had been diagnosed with cancer soon after my family had been obliged to leave France and move back to the United States.

Our return to the States had been precipitated by the completion of my husband's work assignment. I had left France reluctantly, sure that the girl from Montségur would abandon me, sure that once I had left Occitania, the land of the Cathar, the amazing spiritual journey I had been on would come to an abrupt end. I felt certain that I would lose my connection to the ancient spiritual path, lost again in the superficial materialism of the American way of life. I feared that I would return to the person I'd been before moving to France, an active participant in a world consumed by money, entertainment, occasional Sunday church services, and an aching, indefinable emptiness.

But because I was unwilling to return to a life devoid of a spiritual connection, and could no longer turn to the Catholic Church for inspiration, not knowing what else to do, I began to write all that had happened to me. Every morning, before anyone else in the house had awakened, I rose and wrote down all I could remember of my experiences in France.

To my great relief I found that writing kept the channel open and the girl from Montségur stayed with me. Then out of nowhere I was diagnosed with a life threatening cancer. When I began my treatments, all through the shock, the pain, the uncertainty and the confusion, I held tightly to my writing time as if it and only it had the power to safe my life.

"I am a therapist," I told Hau.

"No," she said brushing off my reply. "It's something else. What else do you do?"

I laughed, wondering where she was going with this. "Well," I offered, "I spend a lot of time writing,"

"Yes, said Hau, letting me know with absolute certainty that we were on the right path now. "And what is it you write about?"

I didn't know how to explain it simply. "A group of medieval heretics who lived in what is now the south of France," I said tentatively.

"That's it!" said Hau, as if everything now made sense to her. "You write about the Cathar."

I was stunned. Since returning to the States I hadn't found a single person who knew anything about the heretics.

"You've heard of the Cathar?" I asked in disbelief.

"Of course, I have family in the south of France. I visit often. It's where I buy my lavender," replied Hau, holding up a bottle for me to see. "Each time you come," she continued, "I am left wondering who the crowd is that accompanies you."

"What?" I asked, not trusting what she was implying.

"Now I know it is the Cathar who are with you. And that they have asked you to be their voice. Do you understand? You must write their story. They have asked you to clear their name. As they have assisted in your spiritual initiation, they wish you to tell their story to help others let go of the untruths that have left so many feeling empty, depressed and hungry for spirituality. And from your writing will come your complete healing."

I don't think Hau expected me to respond to what she said to me. And I didn't. In fact that day was the last time we spoke together about the Cathar.

But the conversation with her left me feeling as if I had once again come into direct contact with the mysterious force that had been guiding me since my first encounter with the heretics at Montségur. Hearing Hau's words had given me the same sense of strange excitement that meeting the woman at the night market and the woman on the Labyrinth in Chartres had. While my initial reaction in all these situations was to dismiss what had occurred, my journey had taught me to pay close attention. My journey had taught me that guidance along the path often comes from unlikely sources and more importantly that guidance always comes.

So, while Hau and I never again spoke about the Cathar, I continued to write. I continued also to feel a profound affinity with the Trencavel's of Carcassonne, Esclarmonde de Foix, the Counts of Toulouse and with the enchanted land once called Occitania.

It is my greatest hope and my intention that this story will ignite in others a desire to question what they have been taught, and to examine how those teachings have either assisted or prevented them from establishing and maintaining a deep, sacred and personal connection with the Mysteries.

It is also my hope that *In Secret and Shadows* will inspire in others, as the story of the Cathar inspired me, to embark on a Grail Quest of their very own.

June 7, 2010
San Jose, California

FURTHER READING

Aué, Michele. *Cathar Country*

Aubarbier, Jean-Luc, Binet, Michel, Bouchard, Jean-Pierre.
Wonderful Cathar Country

Baigent, Michael, Leigh, Richard and Lincoln, Henry.
The Holy Blood and the Holy Grail

Baigent, Michael and Leigh, Richard. *The Temple and the Lodge*

Bamford, Christopher, Critchlow, Keith. *Homage to Pythagorus*

Begg, Ean. *The Cult of the Black Virgin*

Bely, Lucien. *The Cathars*

Bokenkotter, Thomas. *A Concise History of the Catholic Church*

Campbell, Joseph. *The Hero with A Thousand Faces*

Charpentier, Louis. *The Mysteries of Chartres Cathedral*

Eisler, Riane. *The Chalice and the Blade*

Fanthorpe, Lionel and Patricia. *Secrets of Rennes le Château*

Hall, Manly P. *The Sacred Teachings of all Ages*

Heartsong, Claire. Anna, *Grandmother of Jesus*

Hoeller, Stephan. *Gnosticism, The Gnostic Jung*

Kingsley, Peter. *Reality*

Marcale, Jean. *Montségur and the Mysteries of the Cathar*

Matthews, John. *The Grail Tradition, Healing the Wounded King*

Motte, Earle. *The Grail Quest*

Pagels, Elaine. *The Gnostic Gospels*

Robinson, James M. *The Nag Hammadi Library*

Roquebert, Michel. *Cathar Religion*

Rouquette, Yves. *Cathars*

Starbird, Margaret. *The Woman with the Alabaster Jar*

Voragine, de Jacobus. *The Golden Legend*

West, John Anthony. *Serpent in the Sky*

ABOUT *the* AUTHOR

JANET PULLEN is a psychotherapist and writer who fell hopelessly in love with the magic and timeless mystery of France during the five years she lived there with her family. An enlightening experience at the mountaintop château of Montségur deep in the foothills of the Pyrénées brought her life into a focus she had not previously imagined possible. Janet has been a student of Kripalu Yoga for over 30 years and is the author of, *Reclaiming the Surrendered Self, When the Spiritual Teacher Betrays the Disciple.* She currently maintains a private psychotherapy practice in the San Francisco Bay and frequently spends time in France.

Breinigsville, PA USA
04 November 2010
248634BV00001B/1/P